€4.50

MAX notes®

Franz Kafka's

Metamorphosis

Text by
Stanley Taikeff
(M. A., Hunter College)
Department of English
CUNY–Laguardia Community College
Long Island City, New York

Research & Education Association

Library of Congress Catalog Card Number 96-67406

International Standard Book Number 0-87891-028-X

MAXnotes® is a registered trademark of
Research & Education Association, Piscataway, New Jersey 08854

What **MAXnotes**® *Will Do for You*

This book is intended to help you absorb the essential contents and features of Franz Kafka's *Metamorphosis* and to help you gain a thorough understanding of the work. The book has been designed to do this more quickly and effectively than any other study guide.

For best results, this **MAXnotes** book should be used as a companion to the actual work, not instead of it. The interaction between the two will greatly benefit you.

To help you in your studies, this book presents the most up-to-date interpretations of every section of the actual work, followed by questions and fully explained answers that will enable you to analyze the material critically. The questions also will help you to test your understanding of the work and will prepare you for discussions and exams.

Meaningful illustrations are included to further enhance your understanding and enjoyment of the literary work. The illustrations are designed to place you into the mood and spirit of the work's settings.

The **MAXnotes** also include summaries, character lists, explanations of plot, and section-by-section analyses. A biography of the author and discussion of the work's historical context will help you put this literary piece into the proper perspective of what is taking place.

The use of this study guide will save you the hours of preparation time that would ordinarily be required to arrive at a complete grasp of this work of literature. You will be well prepared for classroom discussions, homework, and exams. The guidelines that are included for writing papers and reports on various topics will prepare you for any added work which may be assigned.

The **MAXnotes** will take your grades "to the max."

Dr. Max Fogiel
Program Director

Contents

**Each part includes List of Characters,
Summary, Analysis, Study Questions and
Answers, and Suggested Essay Topics.**

Introduction

The Life and Work of Franz Kafka

The oldest of six children, Franz Kafka was born in Prague, Czechoslovakia on July 3, 1883, the son of prosperous, middle-class parents, Hermann and Julie Löwy. Kafka's childhood and adolescence were dominated by his father, a successful merchant who owned a dry goods business. Kafka's father's powerful influence and often tyrannical presence marked Kafka's life both as an artist and as a man. The struggle to free himself from his overbearing father found expression in his fiction as the shy, passive, sensitive victim who suffers and struggles against authoritarian forces and figures. In his *Letter to His Father* (1919), Kafka wrote: "My writing was all about you."

After completing his elementary and secondary education, Kafka graduated from the German University of Prague with a degree in law. Always an avid reader, Kafka was drawn to philosophy and literature, and he soon started to write his own sketches and stories. Among his favorite writers were Dickens, Göethe, Flaubert, Kleist, Thomas Mann, and the Danish philosopher Kierkegaard, the founder of modern existentialism, a philosophy that emphasizes the individual as an agent responsible for his own choices in life.

In 1902, Kafka met the writer Max Brod, who became his close friend, admirer, and biographer. The two young men shared a passion for literature, and they often traveled together in the early years of their friendship. In 1908, Kafka began working for the Workman's Accident Insurance Company in Prague, a government job that would later provide him with material for two of his unfinished novels, *The Trial* (1915) and *The Castle* (1921).

In 1912, an important year in Kafka's life, Kafka met Felice Bauer. Kafka was engaged to her twice during a five-year period, but never married her. During this year, he also finished two important works, *The Judgment* and *Metamorphosis*. Both stories focus on the tortured, father–son relationship; in the latter story, the theme of the individual's estrangement from society is given compelling, dramatic expression. This theme occupied Kafka throughout his life, and recurs throughout his mature fiction.

The year 1919 saw three more important works: *A Country Doctor*, *In the Penal Colony*, and the autobiographical document *Letter to His Father*.

In 1924, while receiving treatment for tuberculosis in Merano, Italy, Kafka met the married writer, Milena Jesenka, with whom he had an affair. In 1923, losing his battle with tuberculosis, Kafka met the 19-year-old Orthodox Jewish woman, Dora Dymant. Dora devoted herself completely to Kafka's care and welfare, and they lived together in Berlin until Kafka's death. He died on June 3, 1924 in Kierling, outside Vienna. He was buried alongside his parents in the Jewish cemetery of Prague-Straschnitz. His three sisters all perished in Hitler's concentration camps.

Kafka's influence on twentieth-century literature is both profound and incalculable. The word *Kafkaesque* has passed into the literature to describe an unsettling, disorienting, nightmarish world that is at once both fearful and menacing in its ambiguity and complexity. His haunting, disturbing, and sometimes grotesque images, combined with his struggling but ultimately defeated heroes, defined an age wherein alienated man—the anti-hero—grappling with meaning and justice in an inscrutable world, is denied answers to both.

Historical Background

The years 1880–1914 (1914 marked the outbreak of World War I) were significant in terms of the changes taking place in the arts in Europe. Traditional artistic forms and structures in literature, painting, poetry, music, and the theatre were undergoing innovative, and in some cases, revolutionary change. Romanticism and naturalism in the fields of painting, music, and literature and realism in the theatre spawned other artistic movements: impressionism and cubism in painting, the atonal system in music, dadaism in poetry and art, and expressionism and absurdism in the theatre. Composers like Debussy, Stravinsky, and Schönberg, writers like James Joyce, Alfred Jarry, and Apollinaire, and painters like Henri Rousseau and Piet Mondrian were experimenting with conventional artistic forms and creating newer, more abstract and symbolic works of art. It was into this vital period of dramatic change in the arts that Franz Kafka was born.

In 1883, the year of Kafka's birth, modern Czechoslovakia was part of the Austro-Hungarian Empire. For Kafka, a Jew who wrote his stories and novels in German, living in Prague forced him into a certain kind of social and cultural isolation. He was not an observant, Orthodox Jew and was therefore estranged from his own people. And since he considered himself a German in language and culture, he was alienated from the Czech people, who comprised the majority of people living in the country. This sense of cultural and societal estrangement was keenly felt by Kafka and it influenced his thought and outlook and contributed to his artistic expression as a writer.

At the age of 28, Kafka wrote in a letter, "I am separated from all things by a hollow space, and I do not even reach to its boundaries." Prague—with its old, crooked streets and ancient, medieval buildings, with its diverse population of Czechs, Germans, Rumanians, and Jews—fed Kafka's imagination from his birth to his death. It was into that "hollow space" that he placed his tormented, alienated characters.

The theme of the artist as an "outsider," cut off from every day reality to create his own transcendent reality, is seen in German literature from Goethe's *Tasso* to Thomas Mann's *Tonio Kröger*. Kafka's own fiction continues in this tradition, but whereas Mann gives us a reality that is recognizable and familiar to us, Kafka's world is more opaque, symbolic, and dream-like in quality, often defying interpretation itself. Like the hero K. of the novels *The Trial* and *The Castle*, we find ourselves struggling to gain a foothold in vastly unfamiliar territory that is both treacherous and terrifying to negotiate.

Hermann Hesse, a German writer and contemporary of Kafka, called Kafka "The uncrowned King of German prose." Kafka's prose style shares the simplicity, clarity, and logic of other German writers, namely, the brothers Grimm and E.T.A. Hofmann. But Kafka's art, with its emphasis on symbol and on the juxtaposition of the real and the fantastic, the rational and the irrational, the ordinary and the extraordinary is unmistakably modern in its sensibility, themes, and vision of the future.

Master List of Characters

Gregor Samsa—*the protagonist or hero of the story.*

Mr. Samsa—*the protagonist's father; an old man, described as having bushy eyebrows and black eyes.*

Mrs. Samsa—*the protagonist's mother; she suffers from asthma and is anxious to please her husband.*

Grete—*the protagonist's younger sister; 17 years old, she plays the violin.*

Chief—*the protagonist's boss; although he is never seen in the story, he is much on Gregor's mind in the early part of the story.*

Chief Clerk—*a bureaucrat representing the Chief.*

Anna—*the 16-year-old servant girl.*

Household Cook—*the woman who asks to be dismissed from her job.*

Three Lodgers—*the three bearded men who rent a room in the Samsa apartment.*

Cleaning Woman (Charwoman)—*the woman who takes on the job of cleaning out the protagonist's room in Part Three.*

Summary of the Novel

Gregor Samsa, a traveling salesman, awakes one morning to find out that he has been transformed into a gigantic insect. From his bed, he looks around his room, adjusting physically and mentally to his new body and wondering if he hasn't been dreaming. But when he tries to turn over onto his right side and can't, he realizes that it is no dream, that indeed he is an insect, complete with a hard shell for a back, wriggling legs, and feelers.

He wants to go back to sleep, but he remembers that he has to get up for work and is already late. His thoughts turn to his job and to the work he does. He hates his job, and he dislikes the Chief of the company. Five years before, Gregor's father's business failed, and Gregor has been supporting his parents and his sister ever since. He has also been paying off his parents' personal debts to the Chief, and he hopes one day to quit his job, settle his parents' accounts, and send his sister to the Conservatory to study music.

While his parents are trying to find out why Gregor hasn't come out of his room, the chief clerk arrives to inquire about Gregor's lateness. When Gregor still doesn't emerge from his room, his parents become worried and send Grete and Anna to get the doctor and locksmith, respectively. The chief clerk threatens Gregor with the loss of his job if he doesn't come out and report for work. Gregor responds by saying that he hasn't been feeling well, but promises to report for work anyway.

When Gregor finally unlocks the door to his room and shows his face, the chief clerk, who is the first to see him, reacts with shock and horror and retreats to the staircase. Mrs. Samsa collapses to the floor at the sight of her son, and Mr. Samsa breaks down and cries. The chief clerk meanwhile is on the landing and wants to flee. Gregor tries to speak to him in order to give him some explanation for what has happened to him, but the clerk flies out of the house. Gregor's father picks up the chief clerk's walking stick, which he left behind, and a rolled newspaper and drives Gregor back into his room. In his panic to escape his father, Gregor gets caught in the door of his room and sustains multiple injuries to himself. Shaken and bleeding, he lies dazed on the floor of his room.

When Part 2 opens, it is twilight of the same day, but we learn later that more time has really elapsed between the morning's events and the time Gregor wakes up again in his room. Grete has taken on the responsibility of feeding Gregor and cleaning out his room, since her parents seem unwilling or unable to cope with the new crisis. The cook implores Mrs. Samsa to let her go. Mrs. Samsa has no choice but to dismiss her, and now Grete must help her mother with the cooking chores as well.

Gregor is able to listen in on his parents' conversation, and he learns that the family has some money left over from his father's investments to live on for about a year. Grete decides that it would be best if much of the furniture is removed from Gregor's room to give him greater freedom of movement. To this end, she enlists her mother's help and the two women start to take out the chest and the writing desk from Gregor's room. When they come back for the picture on the wall, Gregor is clinging tenaciously to it, daring them to take it from him. When Mrs. Samsa sees Gregor spread out on the wallpaper, she shrieks with horror and faints. Grete rushes into another room for something to revive her with. Gregor worriedly follows Grete out, and when the two confront each other, Grete drops a bottle in alarm. The bottle shatters and a sliver of glass cuts Gregor's face. At this point, Mr. Samsa returns to the apartment wearing a blue bank messenger's uniform and cap. When he sees his stricken wife and learns from Grete what has happened, he begins to bombard Gregor with apples. One apple lodges in Gregor's back. Hurt, exhausted, and mortally wounded, Gregor loses consciousness.

Refusing to eat, Gregor is growing weaker and thinner as Part 3 begins. His eyesight is failing him and, because of his injuries— one leg is badly mangled—his movements are severely restricted. The family is now working: Mr. Samsa as a bank messenger, Mrs. Samsa as a seamstress for an underwear company, and Grete as a salesgirl. As Gregor's condition continues to deteriorate, Grete takes less interest in her brother's health and welfare.

Three men come to rent a room in the Samsa apartment. One night after dinner, when Grete is serenading them with her violin, Gregor, who is drawn to the music, sticks his head out his door and is spotted by one of the lodgers. The three men express their outrage and threaten to sue Mr. Samsa for damages. Soon after the men depart to their room, Grete sits down with her parents and urges them to get rid of Gregor.

That night, plagued by guilt, Gregor agrees with his sister that the only solution is for him to disappear. At three o'clock in the morning, he dies.

The new cleaning woman discovers his body. She alerts the Samsas, and then she quickly sweeps up Gregor's corpse. The

Samsa family decides to take a ride in the country. They now pin all their hopes for the future on Grete who, despite her ordeal, has grown into a beautiful, prospective bride.

Estimated Reading Time

Metamorphosis is a comparatively short work, which is divided into three parts of approximately equal length. An average reader, reading 25 pages an hour, should be able to read the entire work in under three hours. You may want to read each part carefully and slowly at first, and then at a later reading, read the complete work for its continuity and sweep of the action.

Metamorphosis

Part 1, Division 1

New Characters:

Gregor Samsa: *the protagonist or hero of the story*

Mr. Samsa: *the protagonist's father; an old man, described as having bushy eyebrows and black eyes*

Grete: *the protagonist's younger sister; 17 years old, she plays the violin*

Mrs. Samsa: *the protagonist's mother; she suffers from asthma and is anxious to please her husband*

Anna: *the 16-year-old servant girl*

Chief Clerk: *a bureaucrat representing the Chief*

Summary

Although *Metamorphosis* falls neatly into three parts, for the purposes of our discussion, we will divide the work itself into six parts. Part 1, Division 1 covers the action of the story from early morning to the chief clerk's discovery of Gregor Samsa.

When Gregor Samsa awakes one misty, rainy morning in his bed, he is astonished to learn that he has been changed into a gigantic insect. He looks around his room and sees all the familiar sights and objects of his former life as a traveling salesman—the sample cloths laid out on his table, his writing desk and chest, the

ticking alarm clock, the picture of the woman clothed in furs on the wall that he had cut out of a magazine and framed—and comes to the conclusion that he must have been dreaming. When he tries to move around in his bed and over onto his right side, he discovers that what has happened to him is, after all, no dream and that he is indeed a huge insect, with all the physical characteristics of an insect—a hard back, dome-like belly, and numerous legs.

Outside, as the rain beats down on his window pane, Gregor's thoughts turn to his job and to the nature of his work as a salesman. Nevertheless, he is resolved to leave his job one day when he has saved enough money and paid off his parents' personal debts to the chief of the company.

Meanwhile, the clock is ticking away, and Gregor becomes more anxious, fearful and worried since he is now already more than an hour late for work. His anxious parents call out to him through his locked door to find out why he hasn't opened his door and come out for his breakfast. As Gregor decides upon a course of action and how best to leave his bed without injuring himself or making too much noise, the chief clerk of his office arrives to find out why Gregor hasn't reported for work that morning. Gregor fears this man as much as he fears the Chief himself and, when he hears the chief clerk's voice on the other side of his door, his anxiety rises.

Mr. Samsa knocks on Gregor's door, and then Grete calls to him, wanting to know if he's all right and whether or not he needs anything. When Gregor does finally force himself off the bed, he lands on the floor with a crash loud enough to be heard in the next room. The chief clerk reacts with some alarm and then addresses Gregor rather harshly, telling him his work has been less than satisfactory, and that his job is in jeopardy. Gregor weakly responds that he has been ill. He defends his work and service to the company and assures the chief clerk that he is now all right and will be coming out shortly.

When Gregor still doesn't emerge from his room, his parents send Grete and the servant girl, Anna, for the doctor and the locksmith. Resolved to leave his room, since he is now convinced that his family and the chief clerk think there is something wrong with him, Gregor struggles to turn the key in his locked bedroom door, but the effort takes all his strength, persistence, and cunning. He can only manage to turn the key with his teeth, but after a while, he succeeds in opening the door. The chief clerk is the first to see Gregor as he emerges from his room.

Analysis

Since its publication in 1915, *Metamorphosis* has intrigued, troubled, puzzled, astonished, and mystified readers. Part of its universal appeal lies in its very subject matter—a conflicted family that must learn to deal with a strange occurrence within the family. On one level, it is the story about an exploited, grown son's refusal to work and to support his family, to take refuge from the world within the four walls of his room, and to revert back to the almost infantile stage of human development where his family must now care for him. However, such a reading of the story trivializes its themes and reduces the work in its complexity and content. Kafka's method, that of fusing ordinary, everyday events with the fantastic and absurd—a method that has its roots in German literature—forces the reader to reread his works in an attempt to penetrate the core of their meaning and to struggle, like his heroes, through the intricate maze of his world to "see the truth."

The French novelist, Albert Camus, said, "The whole art of Kafka consists in forcing the reader to reread." Thus, the reader, of necessity, is forced to return again and again to Kafka. For just as the shifting and changing angle of light in the Samsa apartment creates new moods and tones within the story, so too does Kafka's use of symbols and his deceptively simple prose style force us to re-enter, reconsider, and re-interpret the characters and events in his stories if we are to gain an understanding of his art.

Metamorphosis is divided into three parts of roughly equal length. Each part ends with a crisis in the hero's life, each catastrophe more terrible than the preceding one. This classical division of the story into "three acts," so to speak, allows the action, tension, and conflicts to rise to their tragic climax. Further, all three parts are thematically related: the first part ends with the physical injuries, humiliation, and weakening of Gregor's body; the second part concludes with a more serious and life-threatening injury—the embedded apple in Gregor's back—and further disgrace and

humiliation; and the final part climaxes with Gregor's death after a long, lingering illness.

In this respect, the structure of *Metamorphosis* follows the outlines of classical or Greek tragedy, where we often see the protagonist waging a battle for survival against impossible odds, only to perish at the end. Like Oedipus, who leaves his once ravished city of Thebes restored to health after his punishment and exile, Gregor's death enables his family to return to a normal, natural life after his self-sacrifice.

While many critics claim that only the text itself has worth when examining an author's work, and that any external influences, such as the author's life, are irrelevant to an understanding and appreciation of that text, it is important to mention Kafka's autobiographical *Letter to His Father* in any discussion of *Metamorphosis*. While this very personal document was written seven years after *Metamorphosis*, it is revealing and compelling evidence of the many childhood grievances Kafka held against his father well into adulthood. Near the end of the letter, Kafka takes on his father's voice, allowing him to defend himself against his son's accusations: "I admit we fight each other, but there are two kinds of fight. There is the chivalrous fight, where two independent opponents test their strength against each other, each stands on his own, loses for himself, wins for himself. And there is the fight of the vermin, which not only bite but at the same time suck the blood on which they live."

There is more than a striking parallel in the way Kafka's repressed emotions and inner thoughts surface in this scathing letter to his father and the way Gregor, the verminous insect, reveals his personality and his very private thoughts to the reader after his transformation. Indeed, the entire story may be read and understood as the unmasking of Gregor's ambivalent and conflicted feelings toward his father, and his futile attempts to win his father's love and to settle accounts with him once and for all. As the dutiful, hard-working son, Kafka could not do this, but as a repellent insect, Gregor Samsa can vent his feelings and express his rage and the bile that has been stored up in his heart for so long.

We know that Kafka fought a life-long battle for his father's approval and that as a child, adolescent, and even as an adult, his father made him feel insignificant and worthless, like "vermin." The picture that Kafka draws of his father in *Letter to His Father* is of a brutish man who often ruled the household like a tyrannical bully. Coarse and self-centered, Hermann Kafka seized every opportunity to belittle his son's achievements, accomplishments, and attempts at literature. And while it's true that there is much in Kafka's *Letter to His Father* that is exaggerated, it is also safe to say that the many psychological and emotional indignities and wounds inflicted on Kafka's psyche as a child by his father found their way into the son's fiction and were projected onto his story of the bloodsucking, parasitic son in *Metamorphosis*.

From the very famous, opening sentence, when Gregor Samsa wakes to learn that he has been changed into a "gigantic insect," the reader must suspend his disbelief and enter Gregor's world, accepting what has happened to Gregor as readily as he accepts the fact that the rain is falling outside the Samsa's apartment. Kafka does not explain how Gregor's metamorphosis has come about, and he gives us no clues. Gregor is not hallucinating, and his imagination is not playing tricks on him either. The metamorphosis simply happens and, given the way the story naturally unfolds, it seems as natural and as logical as if Gregor had awakened with a terrible migraine headache or throbbing toothache.

Gregor himself seems, after the initial shock, least troubled by what has happened to him. Soon after he surveys his familiar room, his thoughts immediately turn to his work as a traveling salesman. "Oh, God," he thinks, "what an exhausting job I've picked on! Traveling about day in, day out." His anxiety and fear are not rooted in his sudden transformation, but are centered around his job and the chief clerk! Gregor's "uneasy dreams," the "faint, dull ache," he experiences in his side, "something he had never felt before," his "melancholy" when he turns his head toward the window and sees "the overcast sky," the "small aches and pains" he often felt when lying in bed and that proved to be "purely imaginary" when he got up, the "severe chill" and "change in his voice" can all be regarded as symptoms of his illness before his metamorphosis and directly related to his life as a traveling salesman, but they do not account for his abrupt transformation. These physical details about Gregor's condition are interesting because they point to one of the major

themes of the story—the gradual disintegration and decay of a living organism in the midst of his family's complacent well-being.

The painstaking detail Kafka uses to describe Gregor's room and the Samsa apartment in general contrasts with the everyday, banal levels of existence with Gregor's own fantastic life.

Gregor's room, though small, is clean and neat in the beginning of the story and everything is in its place. We learn that it contains many things that Gregor has lived with for years—his bed, a chest, a ticking alarm clock, a table that holds his cloth samples, the window that looks onto the narrow street and gives onto a hospital, the gilt-framed picture of the woman he had snipped out of a magazine, and a sofa, which is mentioned later in Part 2.

These familiar objects establish Gregor's human existence before his metamorphosis, and they take on greater importance later on in the story when some pieces of furniture are removed from his room, leaving it virtually empty and making his loneliness and isolation from his family and the human community that much more acute and painful.

Early on in Part 1, Gregor begins to think of his life as a traveling salesman, a theme that is taken up again in the latter part of Part 1. It is a demanding job that Gregor hates. The constant traveling causes him any number of worries and irritations, and we learn that if not for his parents' debts owed to the chief of the firm and the fact that Gregor has to support his family after his father's business failed five years before, he would have quit long ago. It is a job done out of necessity to keep his family together, but it is nevertheless done grudgingly and unlovingly. It inspires Gregor's hatred and fear, turning him into the family's reluctant breadwinner. Nevertheless, Gregor still hopes that in another five or six years he will have saved enough money to leave his job, settle his parents' debts, and start a new life.

The theme of family responsibility is at the heart of the story. Gregor's responsibilities and obligations to his family are clearly outlined. Not only does he feel the immense weight of these responsibilities and obligations to his family, but his job has produced strange physical symptoms in him as well, symptoms that may have contributed to his 'presentiment,' his feeling that something was going to happen to him.

Since his family is totally dependent on his salary for their very survival, Gregor must respond to the alarm clock without fail. He must not shirk his duties to his firm or family, appear to be listless or lazy, or show up late for his job. He must carry out his obligations like a good, obedient soldier performing his duties.

As Gregor thinks about the time in the future when he will be able to leave his job, he is instantly aware that he is already very late for work and that he must get up if he is to catch the next train. Gregor's sense of responsibility is brought home to him when he hears his mother's gentle voice calling to him from outside his room, and then his father begins to knock on his door. Finally, his sister, Grete, joins in, plaintively asking Gregor if he's feeling well or if there is anything she can give him. Gregor makes a determined effort to rise from his bed, but the effort to do so proves to be more painful and difficult than he imagines.

While Gregor is thinking about the best way to fling himself off his bed so as not to arouse too much anxiety and terror in the next room, should his parents hear him crash to the floor, the doorbell rings. Gregor instantly stiffens with fear, and he knows that his office has sent someone to his apartment to check up on him. As soon as Gregor hears the visitor's voice, he knows it's the chief clerk, a petty bureaucrat from his firm.

Gregor's thoughts grow dark with foreboding. He seems both humiliated and outraged that the Chief had to send the chief clerk himself to inquire about his lateness, and not some apprentice or minor functionary. Is Gregor's fear of the Chief and the chief clerk unfounded and irrational? Kafka makes it clear that Gregor suffers from more apprehension and dread when the chief clerk arrives than he does when he makes the discovery that he is an insect! In five years of service to the firm, Gregor has never missed a day! He has worked hard, brought money into the firm, and fulfilled his responsibilities to the letter, and yet, what he's most worried about is the office, the Chief, and the chief clerk. "What a fate," he broods, "to be condemned to work for a firm where the smallest omission at once gave rise to the gravest suspicion!"

The stultifying and unrewarding job has condemned Gregor to a death sentence, where the slightest deviation from the rules is looked upon with the most serious consequences by the chief of

the office. This theme of the innocent condemned to a fate worse than death is seen in much of Kafka's work; his novel, *The Trial*, giving it perhaps its most compelling and comprehensive expression. Gregor Samsa, the good, loyal, and obedient son is being punished for his father's financial failure in life. He is trapped, unable to free himself from a position imposed upon him by his father's defeat and insolvency. Like the cornered insect that he has become, Gregor shivers and trembles at the mere sound of the chief clerk's voice, and that voice is enough to propel him off the bed and onto the floor, where he lands with a "loud thump."

While acting in the capacity of a messenger boy for the Chief, the chief clerk is also one more authority figure that Gregor has to contend with. When Gregor's father tells the chief clerk that his son is probably not well and that is the only excuse for his son's not catching the early train, the chief clerk brushes off the excuse by replying that business must be "attended to," and that illness is really no excuse for missing a train. Since Kafka does not describe the chief clerk in any detail, we can only assume that he is a symbol of that world of business and commerce that has "condemned" Gregor to his terrible fate as a salesman. Further, the chief clerk, because of his position in the firm, is another threatening father figure that Gregor must confront, a man who symbolizes the hierarchy of power within the company—Gregor's superior, a man who literally holds his fate in his hands.

And it is exactly because the chief clerk wields that kind of power over Gregor that he launches into a long diatribe, reminding Gregor of his responsibilities to the firm and impatiently demanding to know why he is worrying his parents by barricading himself inside his room. He asks Gregor for an immediate explanation of his stubborn reluctance to show his face. The chief clerk also informs Gregor that the firm has been unhappy with his work and that there is a good chance that he may be fired.

In defense, Gregor tries to explain that he has suffered a minor setback, some mild indisposition that he felt was coming on, but that he is now quite all right and will be coming out in a few minutes. His speech is incoherent, and in his agitated condition, he begs the chief clerk not to implicate his parents in this whole business. "Oh, sir," he cries, "do spare my parents." And he tries to tell him that his reproaches and threats are unwarranted; that, in fact, he has brought in a lot of money and business to the firm. Gregor asks the chief clerk to speak to the Chief about him and to reassure him that he will be reporting for work very shortly.

Fearing that Gregor is very sick, Mrs. Samsa sends Grete to fetch the doctor, while Mr. Samsa, equally disturbed by Gregor's strange behavior, orders the servant girl, Anna, to get the locksmith. The chief clerk, in the midst of all this confusion and panic, remarks of Gregor's voice, "That was no human voice"—a jarring note that at once suggests the extremity of the situation for Gregor's parents and heightens the suspense of the story by exposing Gregor's inhumanity to the social community.

At this point, the reader is made fully aware of Gregor's terrible plight. He is unable to establish human contact through language with the outside world. His voice sounds unnatural, even bizarre and grotesque and shockingly inhuman to the chief clerk.

Throughout the story, we see Gregor struggling toward two contradictory goals: complete and total withdrawal and isolation brought about by his own metamorphosis and his need to be understood and loved by his family, coupled with a desire to be part of the human community. This tug of war in his heart also expresses the ambivalence he feels in his heart. It is poignantly dramatized when Gregor speaks and realizes that although his words are "no longer understandable," his parents now recognize that there is something very seriously wrong with him and are making preparations to help him. "He felt himself drawn once more into the human circle, and hoped for great and remarkable results from both doctor and locksmith, without really distinguishing precisely between them."

The doctor and the locksmith are both seen as Gregor's saviors, the doctor because he heals the sick and the locksmith because he has the tools to free Gregor from his imprisonment, that is, his room. That Gregor can still hope for "salvation" from the outside world means that he sees a way out of his predicament. His desire to rejoin his family again and to return to his job tells us that he has not yet fully resigned himself to his insect life, that once help arrives he will be "saved" and his former life restored to him. This is ironic, for on the one hand, Gregor loathes his job and hopes

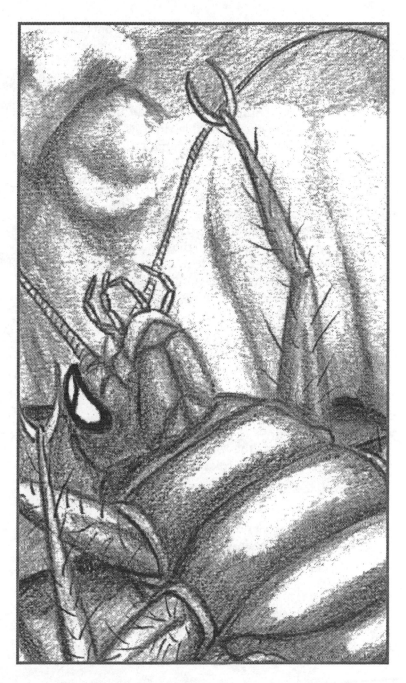

to leave it one day, and, on the other hand, he cries out to be helped, rescued, and saved—to be returned to his normal, mundane life as a salesman.

Because of this apparent contradiction, some critics believe that Gregor's metamorphosis is nothing more than his fantasy to free himself from his boring life as a salesman and to retreat from the world, with all its cares and troubles, into his own cocoon where he forces the world to take notice of him (the Chief and the chief clerk obviously take him for granted). It is from this cocoon that he can safely denounce that world by venting his innermost thoughts and feelings; something, of course, he cannot do as a salesman, or as the obedient son providing for his family. This interpretation would be fine if Gregor awoke from his fantasy, but the events in the story do not support it. In fact, the plot builds away from that interpretation through every incident and scene of the story. Rather than awaken from his fantasy-nightmare, Gregor plunges deeper and deeper into it, sealing his fate and forever changing the lives of his family.

Once Gregor opens the door and reveals himself to his parents and to the chief clerk in order to find out what they think of him, all his hopes for a successful resolution to his situation fade. Appalled and shocked, the chief clerk rears back in fear and horror when he sees Gregor.

Study Questions

1. What are Gregor's thoughts and impressions when he wakes up to find himself transformed into an insect?

2. What kind of work did Gregor do before his metamorphosis?

3. What are Gregor's obligations to his family before his transformation into an insect?

4. What are some of the things that Gregor hopes for?

5. Who sends Grete to get the doctor? The locksmith?

6. How would you describe the chief clerk?

7. What two contradictory goals does Gregor seem to be striving for throughout the story?

8. Why does Gregor finally decide to reveal himself to the chief clerk and his parents?

9. How does the chief clerk threaten Gregor?

10. What is the chief clerk's reaction when he sees Gregor?

Answers

1. Gregor at first seems a little surprised and thinks he may have been dreaming, but as he looks around his room and feels the strange sensations of his new body, he realizes that he has not been dreaming—that he is indeed an insect.

2. Gregor worked as a traveling salesman.

3. Gregor is the sole support of his family before his metamorphosis. He paid the rent, all the bills, and he was paying off his parents' private debts to the chief of his firm.

4. Gregor hopes one day to leave his job for good. His fondest wish is to send his sister, Grete, to music school to study the violin. He hopes to free himself from all his family's obligations and from his parents' dependency on him.

5. Mrs. Samsa sends Grete for the doctor, while Mr. Samsa sends the servant girl, Anna, for the locksmith.

6. The chief clerk is a serious man, all business. He doesn't tolerate any nonsense and seems humorless, threatening, and two-dimensional.

7. Gregor seems to want to withdraw from the world and to be isolated from it, while at the same time he has an irrepressible need to be loved and understood.

8. He wants to see their reaction and is curious to know what they'll say about him.

9. He tells Gregor that his work has fallen off and that he is in jeopardy of losing his position with the firm.

10. The chief clerk is speechless and reacts with shock and horror.

Suggested Essay Topics

1. Write an essay showing the kinds of details Kafka uses to establish Gregor's life before his metamorphosis into an insect. How do these familiar details and objects define Gregor's character and life?

2. As soon as the chief clerk arrives in the Samsa apartment, Gregor reacts with alarm and fear. Write an essay explaining why Gregor stands in such fear of this man, who seems to be nothing more than the chief's messenger.

Part 1, Division 2

Summary

The chief clerk leaps back in fright and shock, with one hand clasped to his gaping mouth. Then Gregor's mother notices him and her reaction is swift and certain: she falls to the floor in a heap, holding her grief-stricken face in her hands. Mr. Samsa can only look on and cry when he sees his unrecognizable and repulsive son.

Realizing that he must do something to explain himself to the chief clerk, Gregor follows him to the stairway in an attempt to reason with him and to calm his fears. However, as soon as he tries to open his mouth to speak, the chief clerk runs out of the house, forgetting his walking stick in the apartment.

As Gregor's mother recovers and straightens up, she accidentally knocks over the coffee pot standing on the breakfast table. The coffee spills all over the floor. The sight of the spilled liquid causes Gregor to snap his jaws together repeatedly, and this inhuman, repugnant sound so frightens Mrs. Samsa that she rushes with a howl into the waiting arms of her husband, who glowers steadily at Gregor.

Gregor's father, who seems both astonished and angry, picks up the chief clerk's walking stick and a rolled up newspaper and begins to drive Gregor back into his room. Panic-stricken, Gregor falls back and away from his enraged father, and when he turns in the doorway of his room to escape his father's wrath, his body gets caught in the frame. His helpless legs can only flutter wildly in the

air while "horrid blotches" ooze from his injured flank. His torment is finally ended when Mr. Samsa gives him one sudden, swift shove into his room.

The door slams behind Gregor, and the silence of the room engulfs him.

Analysis

The way Gregor's parents and the chief clerk respond when they finally see Gregor's unnatural and grotesque body—shock and horror, pain and sorrow, grief and despair, respectively—illuminate the human range of response to anything that is unfamiliar, unnatural, strange, bizarre, and unexpected. Such human responses seem natural enough, for how else can these people react to the sight of their transformed son and business employee? Does Gregor have some perverse motive in showing himself to his parents and the chief clerk? Does he want to shock them out of their hum-drum, everyday life experience? The scene provides the reader with an element of the absurd and the comic. The incongruity of Gregor finally placing himself within sight of everyone concerned about his welfare is so stark and extraordinary and so innocent in its intention, that the spectators who view him naked as an insect have no immediate verbal response, are unable to articulate their feelings, and can only express them on Gregor's own level, that is, demonstratively.

Mr. Samsa's tears perhaps tell us more about his initial response than ordinarily meets the eye. In that one startled glance at his son, doesn't he also see in a flash the loss of Gregor's job and income and the end of the very comfortable life that has sustained him and his family for the past five years? Is he not weeping for his own life and for that of his wife and daughter who now face poverty, illness, and even worse?

For his part, Gregor remains relatively calm after revealing himself. Part of him, of course, has not been altered. The human in him reaching out to others for acceptance and understanding, the need to explain himself fully, to try to apologize to his parents for any inconvenience he may have caused them—all of this is still very much alive in him and is directly connected to his human capacity for feeling, guilt, and remorse. It shows us that Gregor, in his changed state, is opening his heart and soul to his family in ways that he was incapable of doing before his metamorphosis. This is a sign of health and growth, and one of the more fascinating aspects of the story is to see this understanding and love blossom in Gregor even as his physical self begins the long process of decline, decay, and disintegration.

After his appearance in the doorway, Gregor notices that the fog of early morning has lifted and given way to stronger light, and that on the other side of the street, the hospital has come into sharper focus. He also notices the breakfast table with the morning's dishes piled on it, and a photograph on the wall taken when he was in the army. These familiar sights are always in and out of Gregor's vision. More than just connecting Gregor to his human past and to his former life as a salesman, they keep him grounded in everyday, ordinary life as well. Without these banal details, the story would lose much of its power and mystery, for only by placing Gregor within the human context does his appalling situation take on the pain, anguish, and suffering necessary for the tragic quality and dimension he ultimately achieves.

Gregor cannot explain his parents' violent reaction. He still regards himself as their flesh and blood, as a member of the family, and he expects them to treat him like their son. In his mind, he is still Gregor Samsa and he believes that what has happened to him is temporary and will soon pass. He's aware that his physical exterior has changed and that he must look different to everyone, but his heart has remained the same, his ability to think clearly has not been altered, and he is still capable of making his own decisions and of forming his own judgments. That these two parts of the whole—the changed external appearance and his human internal self—can never fully be reconciled (except in death), and accounts for the aching pathos and even humor in the story, and for its inevitable tragic outcome.

Gregor's pressing need to explain himself to the chief clerk—a monologue that never reaches the clerk's ears—is thwarted by the chief clerk's desire to flee the apartment. Gregor's speech allows him finally to express his true feelings about his job and the people he works with without restraint. He reminds the chief clerk that as a traveling salesman, he is often the target of vicious rumors and

attacks. He begs the chief clerk to have some compassion for him. "Don't make things any worse for me than they are," he says. "Stand up for me in the firm." Elsewhere, Gregor says, "I have to provide for my parents and sister."

Gregor fully realizes what the loss of his job would mean for his family. When the chief clerk runs to the staircase, Gregor's sense of alarm and panic intensifies. He knows he cannot allow the chief clerk to vanish without offering him some explanation for what he has just seen. Just as Gregor presses forward toward the chief clerk, his mother springs up from the floor crying out, "Help, for God's sake, help!" In her confusion and panic, Mrs. Samsa accidentally knocks over the coffee pot, spilling coffee all over the floor. When Gregor reacts by loudly snapping his jaws, his mother screams and flies into the outstretched arms of Mr. Samsa. Gregor's plaintive, forlorn "Mother, Mother," is not heard, but the wrenching cry of the heart is the cry of the guilty, responsible son who wants to do right, but who seems crushed and impotent in view of his stricken mother's wailing.

Gregor's attempts to flee his father's wrath are greatly impeded by his inability to move backwards, something he must now do if he is to escape his father's gathering fury. Since he cannot move fast enough in this fashion, though, he has no choice but to swing himself around into a forward position and head straight for his room. He is finally able to do this but only at a great cost to his body. While trying to turn in the doorway, he gets caught. One leg is horribly damaged, fluid oozes from his bruised side, and it is only Mr. Samsa's brutal, violent push that finally frees him from his agony.

This scene is both heartless and cruel. We see the enraged, overpowering, and punitive father with a walking stick in one hand and a rolled newspaper in the other, driving Gregor back into his room. In Mr. Samsa's eyes, Gregor is nothing but a weak, puny, disgusting thing, too small to defend himself. In real life, Kafka wrote about his feelings of insignificance and inferiority in the face of his father's dominance, and how he was made to feel awkward and inadequate in his father's presence. One such passage from *Letter to His Father* reveals how uncomfortable Kafka felt in his father's eyes:

I remember, for instance, how we often undressed in the same bathing hut. There was I, skinny, weakly, slight. You, strong, tall, broad. Even inside the hut, I felt a miserable specimen, and what's more, not only in your eyes, but in the eyes of the whole world, for you were for me, the measure of all things.

Physically, Gregor Samsa is no match for his father. If the father is "the measure of all things," how can a skinny weakling of a son (an insect) ever hope to be his equal or to surpass him in his success and accomplishments in life? Thus Kafka/Samsa (the similar sounding, polysyllabic surnames are obvious in this connection) always felt insecure and inadequate as a man. With the strength of an insect, Samsa could never hope to measure up to his father's tall, massive frame, but would always remain a "miserable specimen" in his father's eyes and in the eyes of the world. Gregor must then resort to other means if he is to survive. He must use other weapons to defend himself—intelligence, cunning, shrewdness, concealment—and since he cannot make himself understood through human speech, he must try to reach his parents in other ways, ways that are inherently doomed to failure.

Though initially appalled and perhaps even repulsed by Gregor's metamorphosis, the reader can only sympathize with Gregor in this final scene of Part 1. Terrorized, Gregor can only stumble and crumble under his father's merciless stamping and the "savage" hissing sounds coming from his throat. When Gregor falls defeated against the doorjamb and is pinned there helplessly with his "dark blotches" staining the white door, the reader immediately grasps the danger and gravity of Gregor's plight and feels both pity and fear for him.

The father's foot-stamping, the ear-splitting hissing sounds coming from his mouth, and the brandishing walking stick and newspaper flying in Gregor's face, foreshadow the more extreme and lethal form of violence seen in Part 2. Mrs. Samsa's own gesture of turning away from her son, toward the open window where she sticks her head out, suggests that the atmosphere in the apartment has suddenly grown oppressive and rank with Gregor's presence. She allows a gust of wind to enter the apartment, a draft that shakes the curtains and scatters the newspaper about the floor.

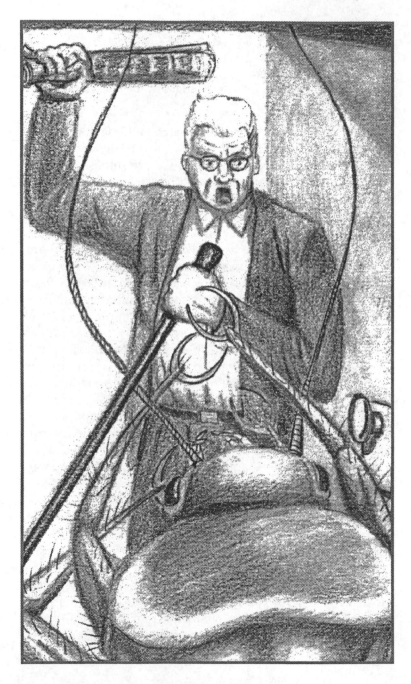

This fresh, cold air "cleanses" and "purifies" the air that has been contaminated by Gregor's noxious appearance in the room. Moreover, the strong light that displaces the heavy mist of morning bursts into the apartment, symbolizing the truth of Gregor's condition, and the change the family must embrace if they are to accept Gregor as their son again.

When the door slams shut behind Gregor and he is once again enveloped in complete silence, we sense that a new phase has opened in Gregor's life and in the life of his family. This is consistent with the major theme of change in the story, for not only has Gregor changed from man to insect, but by the end of Part 1 his parents' lives have been altered. Faced with a threat to their very existence, a threat that is both unfathomable and real to them, their lives have been turned inside out.

From now on, Gregor's physical condition can only worsen, his state of mind grow more melancholy with the passage of time. He had hoped, when he was pulling on the key to his door to free himself from his room, that his parents were outside "pulling for him"; but instead of receiving their encouragement and sympathy, he only succeeded in arousing their fear, hatred, and disgust of him. Their rejection of him as their son is sudden and sure.

The chief clerk's rejection of Gregor is also important. Gregor no longer has any place in society. His job as a traveling salesman defined him in the social community and gave him a certain status among his peers, but now that bond has been severed. His rejection is total. Gregor is an outcast, rejected by his parents and by society. Cut off from everything human, he must now live in isolation, not as a participant in society, but as one of its observers.

One other very important change occurs in Part 1 and that is the complete reversal of roles within the family. For five years, Gregor was able to meet his family's financial obligations, but now all that has changed. Transformed utterly into an insect, he can no longer provide that support for his parents and sister. He is now dependent upon them for his very survival and must now live off them like a parasite, just the way they lived off him and "sucked his blood" for five years. In this, we have the revenge theme, the exploited son who abjures all and any responsibility toward those who had taken unfair advantage of him.

Study Questions
1. How do Mr. and Mrs. Samsa react when they see Gregor for the first time?
2. Why can't Gregor explain himself to the chief clerk?
3. What are some of the things Gregor tries to tell the chief clerk?
4. Who knocks over the coffee pot?
5. What causes Mrs. Samsa to collapse to the floor?
6. How does Mr. Samsa force Gregor back into his room?
7. What happens to Gregor as he is being driven back into his room?
8. In what ways has Gregor been alienated from society?
9. How have the roles within the Samsa family changed?
10. What is the major theme of the story?

Answers
1. Mrs. Samsa collapses on the floor and buries her face on her breast, while Mr. Samsa looks angrily at Gregor and begins to cry.
2. Gregor can't explain himself to the chief clerk because the chief clerk is not listening and because Gregor's speech is unintelligible to him.
3. Gregor tries to remind the chief clerk that he is often the target of unfounded rumors and malicious attacks. He begs the chief clerk to have some compassion for him, and he reminds him that he has to provide for his family's welfare.
4. Mrs. Samsa, in her panic and confusion, knocks over the coffee pot.
5. Seeing Gregor for the first time, Mrs. Samsa at first stares incredulously at him and then falls to the floor.
6. Mr. Samsa chases Gregor back into his room with a walking stick, rolled up newspaper and by stamping his feet and hissing savagely.

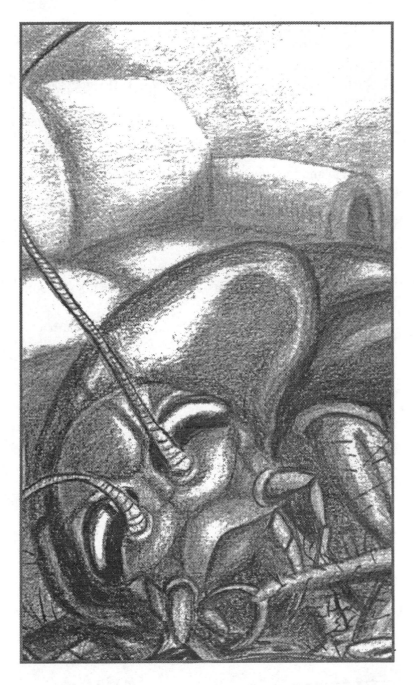

7. Gregor gets caught in the doorway as he is being driven back into his room.

8. Gregor has been rejected by his parents and by the chief clerk, who symbolizes the outside world of business and finance.

9. The roles within the Samsa family have been completely reversed. The parents, who had lived off Gregor for five years, now realize that their helpless son can no longer provide for them and they must find a way to support not only themselves and their daughter, but their son as well.

10. The major theme of the story is change.

Suggested Essay Topics

1. The relationship between Gregor and his father is at the core of the story. Write an essay describing this relationship both before and after Gregor's metamorphosis.

2. During much of this part of the story, we get to learn a lot about Gregor's inner life—his thoughts and feelings. Write an essay describing Gregor's private thoughts and emotions, and explain how these thoughts and feelings express his attitude toward his family and the outside world.

Part 2, Division 1

New Character:

Household Cook: *the woman who asks to be dismissed from her job*

Summary

Part 2, Division 1 covers the action of the story from twilight of the same day to the removal of Gregor's furniture from his room.

When Gregor wakes up it is twilight. He is immediately drawn to the smell of food in his room and sees a basin of milk with little pieces of bread floating around in it. The sight of the food makes him happy because he knows that no one else but his sister, Grete, left it for him and because she knows that milk is his favorite drink. Instead of drinking the milk, however, Gregor discovers that he has lost his appetite for it and he leaves the milk alone. He also discovers that one of his legs is seriously injured, the result of his father's assault on him earlier that morning.

A little while later, when Grete returns to his room to check up on her brother, she notices that the milk is untouched. She removes the basin, goes out, but soon returns with a plate full of vegetables, stale cheese, some dry bread, and raisins. Gregor finds this food more to his liking, and he munches hungrily on the cheese. From then on, Gregor is fed twice a day, once in the morning and then again in the afternoon. Grete becomes chiefly responsible for feeding Gregor and tending to his needs.

The cook begs Gregor's mother to let her leave the house and to quit her job. Her decision is based on the fact that she doesn't want to be around Gregor anymore. She gives Mrs. Samsa her word of honor that she won't say anything to anyone about Gregor. Mrs. Samsa consents and the cook leaves.

Gregor is able to overhear his father in the next room talking to his mother and sister about the family's financial situation. He learns that his father had made some investments years before, and that he still has some money put away that the family can live on for the next year or two.

Gregor's thoughts turn to his former life as a salesman, and he takes pride in the fact that he was able to provide for his family. He also thinks of his former business acquaintances, and he still has the fervent desire to send his sister to the conservatory to study the violin. These thoughts make him a little sad as he listens to his parents and he recalls the glory of his past life.

Grete decides that it would be best for Gregor if some of the furniture in his room was removed. This, she thinks, is in his best interest, for it would allow him greater freedom of movement. Mrs. Samsa, at first, resists Grete's idea but she finally gives in and agrees to help her daughter in this task. Gregor, however, likes his furniture; it reminds him of his past and the warm memories associated with it. When the time comes to remove the furniture, Gregor can only look on helplessly, as his mother and sister begin to take

out the chest and the writing desk. There is, however, one article in the room that Gregor will not let them have and that is the picture on the wall of the woman dressed in furs. Climbing up on the wall, Gregor spreads himself over the glass, fiercely defying his sister and mother to take the picture from him.

Analysis

The time factor in this part of the story becomes a little blurred. Although it is clearly twilight of the same day when Part 2 opens, we learn that, later on, an indefinite period of time will have elapsed, perhaps a few days, perhaps longer; it isn't clear.

In Part 2, Gregor's health begins to deteriorate. He no longer has any taste for his favorite beverage, milk, and his badly mangled leg hampers his movement and virtually turns him into an invalid. The stage is therefore set for his total physical decline and eventual death. Also, his failing eyesight, which suggests a loss of consciousness, and his reluctance to nourish himself, symbolize his steady withdrawal from the world and intensify his alienation from the human environment.

As this section of the story opens, an eerie silence permeates the apartment. In the living room a light is burning, but Gregor notices through a crack in his door that his father is not reading his newspaper aloud, a habit of his that he indulges in every evening. Gregor has an uneasy feeling when he reflects upon the comfortable life he had provided for his family for the past five years. "But what if all the quiet, the comfort, the contentment were now to end in horror," he thinks to himself. Gregor now knows that there's no turning back, that the change in the family roles is irreversible and that he is now completely dependent upon his family for his survival. This thought greatly disturbs him and he begins to crawl back and forth in his room, agitated and depressed.

During the long night, Gregor hides under the sofa in his room. The sofa becomes his safe harbor, his refuge, the one place where he can hide himself from the world. He lies there thinking about how he can best help his family suffer the inconvenience he has caused them. He has troubled and vague thoughts and hope occasionally interrupts his thinking. He resolves to be patient and to wait to see what happens next. These thoughts reveal Gregor's sense of guilt and the profound sense of responsibility he still feels toward his parents and sister. Even in his present condition, he feels that he cannot let them down, and he struggles to find ways to fix things and to accommodate his family.

In the morning, Grete once again enters his room but quickly retreats when she sees him. From under the sofa, Gregor watches her come into the room moments later to pick up the basin of milk and carry it away. She returns presently with other food, this time with a plate of decaying vegetables, raisins, a wedge of hard cheese, a buttered roll, and a basin of water. After Grete leaves, Gregor sniffs at the food and quickly eats the vegetables and the cheese, leaving the fresh food untouched. Since a dung beetle—which is what the cleaning woman in Part 3 calls him—is an insect that feeds on excrement, it is interesting that Gregor now finds no pleasure in fresh food, but is drawn to the old, stale, decaying vegetables and cheese and the sauce coating the old bones—food that is hardly nutritious to sustain him or give him back his strength.

From the opening pages of Part 2, it is clear to the reader that Grete has assumed the major responsibility of caring for her brother. She brings him his food twice a day and when he is finished eating, she picks up the uneaten remains, collects them in a bucket and goes out. She is the only one in the family who has the courage to take care of Gregor. That she still loves her brother is clear from the way she expresses her concern for his health and welfare, but as time passes, her concern diminishes and her attitude toward him changes.

It is clear to Gregor that a wall separates him from his sister. While he knows that Grete can never understand his words, he is struck by the fact that it never occurs to Grete that he can understand her perfectly. All verbal communication between Gregor and his sister is lost, further evidence of Gregor's alienation from his family and his sense of abandonment.

With the doors to his room partially open for him to eavesdrop on his family's conversations in the adjoining room, Gregor soon finds out that the cook has asked his mother to be dismissed. Although the cook never states her reasons for wanting to leave, the reader can only assume that she has found out about Gregor and is both repulsed and frightened by him. Mrs. Samsa grants the

cook's wish, and when the cook takes her departure, she promises Mrs. Samsa not to breathe a word of Gregor to anyone. The cook's desertion from the Samsa household echoes the chief clerk's flight—both running away from the verminous creature hiding in the next room!

With the cook's departure, Grete now has to take on an added burden, that of helping her mother prepare the meals for her family. It is one more thankless job that Grete is burdened with. In a very short period of time, her young life as been turned upside down. She is not only Gregor's caretaker, but she has become his cook and maid as well. She must also exercise extreme prudence and caution whenever she visits him, for although the sight of him no longer alarms her, there is always the possibility that something she does or says in his presence will excite him or irritate him in some way, so she must readjust her behavior and act in a way that is foreign to her, and this helps to change her attitude and personality. These changes in Grete have repercussions for Gregor and for her parents later on in the story when Grete begins to crumble from all the pressure and stress placed on her shoulders. She has replaced Gregor in the family as the exploited child, the child that must now "produce" if the family is to remain strong and healthy. Subtly, Grete is undergoing her own metamorphosis from a young, inexperienced girl of 17 to a young woman fast outgrowing her adolescence by the many roles that have been thrust upon her by Gregor's transformation.

Gregor is able to overhear his father discussing the family's affairs with his wife and daughter. Although Mr. Samsa's business had failed five years earlier, Mr. Samsa, the shrewd businessman, still has some money left over from some investments he made at the time; money enough, he tells his wife for the family to live on for another year or two. This news cheers Gregor. It was because of his father's business failure that Gregor became a traveling salesman in the first place. In the beginning of his new career, Gregor was quite successful and his travels brought a lot of money into the firm. He was able to pay all the household expenses himself. His parents seemed to take his money for granted, getting used to an easy, comfortable, trouble-free life. They never expressed their appreciation and gratitude to Gregor in a way that would have pleased him. When Gregor recalls his former life, it is with a sense of regret and disappointment, not bitterness. Only his sister, he feels, has remained close to him, and it is for this reason that he still thinks of sending her off to the conservatory to study the violin. He wistfully recalls how he had promised himself to do just that and announce his decision to his parents on Christmas Day, as he listens intently to his father discuss the family's financial arrangements in the next room.

Although Gregor is happy to learn that there is money enough for the family to live on for a while, he realizes that his aging father and ailing mother are in no condition to go out and work for a living. His sister, who has had little experience of life, is quite incapable of taking on the responsibility of a job. All her life, Grete has entertained herself with frivolous matters and, with the possible exception of her violin, she has not devoted herself to anything serious. These grim reminders of his family's dire circumstances throw Gregor into turmoil and despair. His guilt gnaws away at him; he is filled with shame and grief for the horrible burden he has placed on his family and he feels most wretched in having disappointed them.

As the days and nights pass, Gregor is slowly losing his ability to see. The hospital outside his window grows dimmer by the day, the view from his window when he gazes through it, seems like a vast expanse of "desert waste," where "grey sky and grey land blended indistinguishable into each other."

Gregor's weak eyesight, his general lassitude, his morbid, afflicted thoughts, his expenditure of effort whenever he pushes the armchair to the window after Grete moves it back into the room, are strong indicators that Gregor's powers are rapidly declining. The "grey sky" and "grey land" suggest that heaven and earth have become one for him, namely, a "desert waste" and nothing more.

Grete's attitude and behavior also show signs of change. When she enters Gregor's room, her movements are impatient and rushed. She can't wait to put down his food and be gone. Her haste and impatience distress Gregor, and he takes to hiding under his sofa with a sheet pulled down over his face, so as not to give Grete too much of his repulsive body to look at. Gregor realizes that the sight of him still disgusts his sister and thinking only of her, he labors for hours to drag the sheet over to the sofa—anything to please her and to spare her anymore discomfort, unhappiness, and displeasure. Here we have the physically repulsive and sorely afflicted Gregor expressing his worry and concern and love for his healthy, young sister who, when she enters his room, displays nothing but her uneasiness and indifference toward her brother.

Gregor's love for Grete is both powerful and undeniable. It connects him to all that is human and divine in life, all that is lasting and eternal. It matters little to him that his love is not returned, for Gregor has always been a loving, self-sacrificing son and brother, sacrificing his time and energy to the firm and family and seeing to it that his elderly parents were comfortable and secure. Not even as an insect does Gregor fail to feel the stirrings of love in his heart. This profound feeling of love and attachment that Gregor feels for Grete propels him toward making the ultimate sacrifice in Part 3.

With the passage of time, Mrs. Samsa grows restless and impatient and wants to see her son. "Do let me in to Gregor," she says, "he is my unfortunate son. Can't you understand that I must go to him?" Grete makes arrangements for her mother to visit Gregor, but before this can be done, Grete feels that Gregor needs more room to move about unhindered and decides to remove most of the furniture from his room. She notices that, among other things, Gregor has taken to climbing the walls and ceiling and that one of his favorite games is to hang suspended from the ceiling. Indeed, Gregor has grown accustomed to his new body, and he has more control over it than before. These acrobatics allow him to rest and relax and to enjoy blissful states of consciousness.

Study Questions

1. Why doesn't Gregor drink the milk his sister leaves for him?
2. Why does the household cook ask Mrs. Samsa to let her go?
3. Where does Gregor like to hide?
4. Who has assumed major responsibility for Gregor's life?
5. Why did Gregor become a traveling salesman?
6. How do the Samsa's expect to live now that their son's source of income is lost?

7. Why is Gregor so intent on sending his sister to the conservatory to study music?

8. In what ways are Gregor's physical powers declining?

9. How has Grete's attitude and behavior toward Gregor changed?

10. Why does Grete want to remove most of the furniture from Gregor's room?

Answers

1. Gregor finds it hard to eat anything with the soreness and tenderness in his side, and the sight of the milk only repulses him, even though it has always been his favorite drink.

2. The cook wants to leave the Samsa household because she no longer wants to work in the same apartment where there is a repulsive creature living.

3. Gregor likes to hide under the sofa in his room because it is a safe place and gives him some protection from the outside world.

4. Grete has assumed the major task of caring for Gregor.

5. Gregor became a traveling salesman after his father's business failed.

6. Mr. Samsa made some investments while he was in business, and the Samsa's can expect to live off this money for a year or two at the most.

7. Gregor feels closest to his sister in the family and his love for her is expressed by his fervent desire to pay for her musical education at the conservatory.

8. Gregor's mobility has been seriously impaired by the injury to one of his legs; furthermore, he is beginning to lose his eyesight. Finally, he is weakened by his efforts to move the armchair to the window every time Grete moves it away.

9. Grete begins to grow impatient whenever she has to enter Gregor's room to feed him and to clean up the room. Her indifference also becomes evident in having to care for

Gregor. While she herself may not be aware of the changes in her character, Gregor perceptively realizes that her enthusiasm and interest in him are waning.

10. Grete feels that Gregor needs more room to move about in and to that end she wants to remove most of the furniture from his room.

Suggested Essay Topics

1. Grete's character undergoes a dramatic change in this section. Trace the changes in her character in an essay that highlights the changes in her attitude, character, and personality.

2. Gregor's furniture is very dear to him and he becomes very upset when Grete and her mother start to remove it from his room. Write a detailed essay explaining why Gregor feels he cannot part with his furniture.

Part 2, Division 2

Summary

Part 2, Division 2 covers the action from the sighting of Gregor on the wall by Mrs. Samsa to Mr. Samsa's bombarding Gregor with apples.

After Grete and Mrs. Samsa remove Gregor's writing desk and place it in the next room along with the other furniture, they start back to his room to see what other pieces they can take out. Gregor is so agitated and distraught over the removal of his furniture that he runs around his room in a panic hoping to save what is left. The picture of the woman on the wall catches his eye and he flies up to it and clings to it tenaciously, determined at any cost to hold onto it.

Grete sees him first as she and her mother re-enter Gregor's room. She tries to shield her mother's eyes from the sight of Gregor spread out against the wall, but when the weary Mrs. Samsa lifts her eyes to the wall and sees Gregor hanging onto the picture, she screams, "Oh, God, Oh, God!" and falls down on the sofa.

Alarmed, Grete runs out of the room and into another room to get something to revive her stricken mother. Worrying that his

mother may be dying, Gregor rushes out of the room and follows Grete, but when the two meet, Grete panics at the sight of him and drops one of the bottles she is holding. A piece of shattered glass cuts Gregor's face. Grete then dashes out of the room, slamming the door behind her, locking Gregor inside.

Presently, Mr. Samsa returns to the apartment. He is dressed in a bank messenger's uniform with gold buttons and a service cap. When he notices his wife sprawled out on the floor, with Grete bending over her, Mr. Samsa demands to know what happened, and when Grete tells him that Gregor has gotten loose in the apartment, he grows enraged and glares at Gregor, who by this time, has freed himself from the room. As soon as Gregor sees the fire in Mr. Samsa's eyes, he retreats to his bedroom.

Driven by a strong desire to punish Gregor for making Mrs. Samsa suffer, Mr. Samsa picks up some apples and starts to throw them at Gregor. One apple grazes Gregor's back and another one finds its mark and sinks deeply into his back.

Mortally wounded, Gregor soon loses consciousness. Before he blacks out, though, he sees his mother pick herself up and fly into Mr. Samsa's arms. With her clothes in disarray, Mrs. Samsa runs terrified and screaming into her husband's comforting embrace and pleads with him to spare her son's life.

Analysis

When the time approaches for Mrs. Samsa and Grete to enter Gregor's room to remove his furniture, Gregor takes refuge under the sofa with the sheet practically covering his entire body. Only his head sticks out from beneath the sofa so he can better observe his mother and sister in the room. For about 15 minutes, the two women struggle to remove the heavy chest, but after a while, Mrs. Samsa has a sudden change of heart. She realizes that by removing Gregor's furniture, they would be showing him that they have given up on him ever returning to normal or improving in any way. Mrs. Samsa still clings to the hope that Gregor will one day get better and she tells Grete that when that day comes, Gregor will want to see the furniture in his room just as it was before his metamorphosis.

Grete, however, still wants the furniture out and, after a heated argument, Mrs. Samsa finally gives in. After the chest is removed, the writing desk is the next piece of furniture to be taken out. Immediately, Gregor reacts to this outrage. His writing desk is something important to him; it holds sweet memories for him when he used to do his homework at it; it represents the toil and labor of his young life in grammar school. It is another strong link to his past that he feels cut off from if it is taken from him. All he could do though is watch as the desk is loosened from the floor and removed and carried out into the adjoining room. Affronted and provoked, Gregor comes out from under the sofa and rushes about the room, wondering what he can salvage and keep from his sister's hands.

Suddenly, the picture of the woman on the wall attracts his attention and he hurriedly crawls up toward it, flattening himself against the glass and adhering to it with his sticky legs. Clinging ferociously to it, he challenges Grete and his mother to take it away from him. This is the first time in the story that we see Gregor asserting himself and fighting for what is rightfully his. This shows us that Gregor is still very much alive, that his will has not been broken. He has suffered both mentally and physically since his metamorphosis, but he will not suffer the loss of his favorite picture, even if it means doing harm to Grete.

The reader must begin to wonder at this point why Gregor feels so strongly about this picture. Who is the woman in it? What does she represent, wrapped in her furs, and why is Gregor so determined to keep it all for himself? The picture may symbolize the eternal image of maternal love for Gregor, or perhaps the woman reminds Gregor of Mrs. Samsa herself, fashionably dressed in expensive furs. Whatever its meaning, the picture is enough to turn Gregor from an accepting, passive observer, to an aggressive, active participant in his own drama, risking everything—life and limb—in that one defiant act of covering the picture with his entire body.

When Mrs. Samsa re-enters Gregor's room with her daughter, she sees her son clinging to the picture. The sight of him like that so frightens her that she falls in a faint on the sofa. Agitated and alarmed, Grete instantly rushes out into another room to get something to revive her mother with. Worried about his mother's frail health, Gregor leaves the wall and runs out after Grete. But when he surprises her and she comes face to face with her brother, Grete

drops one of the bottles she is clutching in her hand and runs out, locking the door behind her. A sliver of glass cuts Gregor's face and now he's shut out once again from his mother and sister. Alone, he thinks his mother may be dying, but there is nothing he can do at this point, and so he waits and tries to calm himself down.

Gregor's father, who has been out of the apartment, now returns. He has found work as a bank messenger and he enters the apartment dressed in his messenger's uniform—a handsome blue uniform with gold buttons and cap. Noticing at once his wife's prostrate body with Grete leaning over her in an attempt to revive her, Mr. Samsa becomes alarmed and frightened and demands to know what happened in his absence. Grete tells him that Gregor has gotten loose. Mr. Samsa is not surprised. He knew that something like this was going to happen some day and now his worst fear has been realized.

Meanwhile, Gregor manages to leave the room. Afraid that his father thinks he's done something monstrous, he tries to return to his room and hides near the door. He shows enough of himself, however, to his father to let him know that he's done nothing wrong, that he's not responsible for Mrs. Samsa's afflicted condition. When Mr. Samsa notices Gregor cowering before him in the doorway, he cries out, "Ah!" in a menacing, angry voice.

Gregor hardly recognizes his father in his new bank uniform. He looks fit and healthy, tall and strong as he comes bearing down on him. The figure of his father now before him—his white hair parted neatly on either side of his head, his sharp black eyes burning into him, his bushy eyebrows—bears little resemblance to the man who was his father when he stayed home and waited for Gregor to return from one of his business trips. The contrast for Gregor is striking and it inspires fear and dread in his heart. Gregor can only try to run out to meet his father in an attempt to pacify him. The two confront one another then circle each other like two antagonists. But again, Gregor can hardly stand up to his father and before long, his breath gives out, and he tries to stagger back to his room.

Several apples begin to rain down on him and only when one grazes his back does Gregor realize that his father is trying to murder him! Another apple gets stuck in his back, and in his feeble attempts to escape the punishing missiles, he falls and lies crushed under the weight of the embedded apple lodged in his back. Out of the corner of his eye, he sees his mother running to his father's outstretched arms, sees her disheveled clothes and their desperate embrace, and then he blacks out.

This is the most harrowing scene in the story, perhaps one of the most brutal and gripping scenes in modern literature. The scene is both arresting and compelling for several reasons: for the understated horror and pain it evokes and for the sheer cruelty it paints of an innocent, defenseless son suffering the undeserved punishment of the powerful, vengeful father.

The sexual symbolism of the scene, with its reenactment of the Oedipus conflict, is all too clear. Here we have the reborn, rejuvenated father returning to the apartment in a position of strength and authority only to witness the sight of his stricken wife down on the floor, her clothing loosened about her body, her flesh exposed, and the frightened, trembling cause of it all hiding behind his bedroom door. Gregor, who had supplanted his father in the household as the breadwinner and therefore as the "surrogate" husband, now finds himself at his father's mercy. Mr. Samsa, who now wears his new uniform on his back like a badge of paternal authority for all to see, must punish his son, the transgressor, the root cause of his wife's shameless suffering. The weak and ineffectual father, who once lounged around the house in his dressing gown waiting for his son to hand him his salary has himself been transformed in Gregor's eyes into a tyrannical monster who now earns his own wages.

Almost from the very beginning of Gregor's metamorphosis, Mr. Samsa has been unwilling to accept Gregor as his son. Mrs. Samsa and Grete have shown a willingness to do just that, but from the start, the father rejected his son and effectively cast him out of his life. Reduced to the verminous form of an insect, Gregor is a constant reminder of the grotesque, weak, and pitiful aberration that Mr. Samsa has sired. And now that Gregor has truly revealed himself in all his audacious and spiteful behavior, Mr. Samsa is driven to destroy him. In his eyes, Gregor has become everything loathsome to him—puny, parasitic, weak, a being clothed in a personality lacking in strength—not the kind of son this once strong, successful, and ambitious storekeeper could be proud of. Mr.

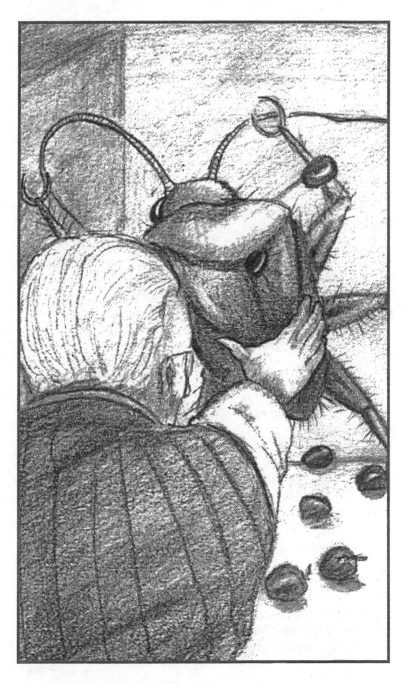

Samsa is a victim of his own drives and obsessions, but it is note-worthy that what sets him on his murderous rampage is the sight of his tearful, helpless wife lying on the floor in nothing but her "underbodice," her petticoats loosened around her, her bare flesh shamefully exposed.

By the end of Part 2, the reader is made aware of the significant changes that have occurred in the lives of the characters. For one thing, Grete no longer shows the same exuberant behavior in caring for Gregor that she did at the beginning of the story. She is unable to bear the full weight of the responsibility that has been thrust upon her as Gregor's servant and maid. The ambivalence she feels is slowly pushing her toward the edge and is forcing her toward some fateful decision.

Mrs. Samsa seems the most torn by Gregor's misfortune. On one level, she is still horrified and repelled by Gregor, but in pleading for her son's life, she demonstrates the love and concern she still has for him as his mother. Her son can provoke her husband's wrath, but she will not allow him to murder him right before her eyes.

Mr. Samsa, on the other hand, is indomitable in his refusal to show the least tenderness, understanding, or sympathy for what has befallen Gregor. And now that Gregor must live off his salary, Mr. Samsa wants him out of the way for good. He has no further use for him since Gregor is no longer any use to the family. Acting as the family judge and jury, Mr. Samsa sentences his son to a certain death.

As for Gregor himself, the most important change is that he is now totally dependent upon his family for his very survival, but most of all upon his father, since it is Mr. Samsa who now wields all the power and influence in the household and who now makes all the important decisions affecting his life.

Helpless, unable to articulate his thoughts and feelings to his father, without love, without any friends, without even his one-time business associates, stripped of his furniture, alone, mortally wounded, Gregor is now at his father's mercy. Reduced by his metamorphosis to living off his parents like a child, Gregor has no escape route, no one to appeal to, and no one to save him.

The rotting apple in his back, which remains embedded in his flesh, is a constant reminder of his father's wrath and cruelty. His powerful, god-like father has cast him out of "Eden" and, with the tossing of the apples, has crushed his failure of a son to earth. Gregor's fate is now sealed.

Study Questions

1. Why does Gregor cling to the picture of the woman in furs on the wall?

2. What causes Mrs. Samsa to faint on the sofa?

3. Why does Gregor run after Grete after his mother faints?

4. What kind of job has Mr. Samsa taken?

5. Why doesn't Gregor recognize his father in his new uniform?

6. How does Mr. Samsa react when he first comes into the apartment and sees his wife lying on the floor?

7. How does Mr. Samsa punish Gregor?

8. Why does Gregor lose consciousness?

9. Who saves Gregor from an almost certain death?

10. How has the balance of power in the Samsa household changed by the end of Part 2?

Answers

1. Gregor feels a certain attachment for this picture. He had cut it out of a magazine and framed it at one time. It is something special for him. The figure of the woman may remind him of his own mother, or it may just give him a sense of warmth and comfort knowing it's there on his wall for him to gaze at.

2. Mrs. Samsa faints when she sees Gregor sprawled out across the picture on the wall.

3. Gregor is worried that his mother may be dying and so runs after Grete to try to help.

4. Mr. Samsa has taken a job as a bank messenger.

5. Gregor hardly recognizes his father at first when he comes into the apartment because he is wearing a blue uniform

and because he looks so unlike the man that he was used to seeing sitting around the house in his dressing gown. The sudden change in his father's appearance jolts Gregor.

6. Mr. Samsa is greatly upset and angry because he knew Gregor would one day get "loose" in the apartment, and now he sees that he was right.

7. Mr. Samsa stones Gregor with apples.

8. One apple gets stuck in Gregor's back. This is a crushing blow and mortal wound. It weakens Gregor, and so he loses consciousness.

9. Mrs. Samsa begs her husband to spare Gregor's life.

10. Now that Mr. Samsa is again earning money, he has the upper hand and is no longer dependent upon Gregor for his comfort and security. And since Gregor is now no longer able to work, he must depend upon his father, and to a lesser degree, upon his sister and mother, for his survival.

Suggested Essay Topics

1. The picture of the woman wrapped in furs on Gregor's wall is something that he refuses to part with. Write an essay showing the importance of this picture in Gregor's life and, if possible, try to explain its symbolic meaning.

2. In this section of the story, Gregor's sense of guilt is highlighted. Write an essay exploring the different things Gregor feels guilty about, and show how his lingering guilt affects his state of mind and his feelings toward his family.

Part 3, Division 1

New Characters:

Three Lodgers: *the three bearded men who rent a room in the Samsa apartment*

Cleaning Woman (Charwoman): *the woman who takes on the job of cleaning out the protagonist's room in Part 3*

Summary

Part 3, Division 1 covers the action from a description of Gregor's worsening physical condition to the concert Grete gives for the three gentlemen lodgers. One month has elapsed from the time Mr. Samsa injured Gregor with the apple.

The apple decaying in Gregor's back has made him extremely weak and has greatly limited his physical movement. He is almost completely incapacitated now, but he can lie in the silence of his room and listen in on the conversations of his parents in the living room since the door to that room is now wide open all the time.

The family has adopted an attitude of patience toward Gregor, and even Mr. Samsa has put aside his feelings of disgust for his son and has resolved to be more patient and to see what happens.

All the family members are now working. Gregor's mother is working for an underwear firm, sewing at home; Grete has taken a job as a salesgirl, and she is also learning French and shorthand in order to secure a more solid future for herself. Mr. Samsa, as has already been noted, works as a bank messenger.

For more than a month, Gregor has been confined to his room. During this time, his room has grown oppressive and filthy; dust is everywhere, on the floor, in the corners, on the walls, and thick dust balls cling to Gregor's body when he drags himself along the floor. His physical appearance is unsightly. He eats very little now and is growing weaker and more frail by the day.

Grete no longer takes any pride in her care for Gregor. She allows his room to grow dirty and stale, if not chaotic with filth. When she has to go into his room to bring him his food, she does so quickly and not without a little contempt. The strain of taking care of her brother for so long has finally caught up with her and has affected her outlook, her spirit, and her personality. Besides, with her new job, she now has other interests and pursuits in life, and so Gregor is no longer the center of her universe.

To help meet the household expenses, the Samsas decide to rent one of the rooms in the apartment to three men. These men are all bearded and appear to be serious in their manner, bearing, and speech. They take their evening meals in the living room and smoke their cigars and read their papers after dinner while the Samsas eat in the kitchen. The three lodgers are obsessed with order and cleanliness, and they demand that the garbage can and ash can be placed in Gregor's room. The Samsas have also dismissed Anna, the young servant girl, and in her place have hired an old cleaning woman to come into the apartment in the morning and evening to help with the domestic chores. This old woman complies with the lodgers' demands and dumps the refuse cans in Gregor's room.

One evening, after dinner, Grete is playing her violin in the kitchen. The music casts a spell over the apartment and the three lodgers stop what they are doing to listen. Gregor too is attracted to the sad, graceful melody coming from the kitchen. He crawls to the doorway of his room and sticks his head out into the living room where he is mesmerized by the music.

Analysis

Gregor's disabling injury—the rotting, festering apple sinks deeper and deeper in his back for everyone to see—makes it virtually impossible for him to crawl on the walls or the ceiling and reduces him to the status of a crippled invalid. Perhaps feeling a little guilty himself for inflicting this horrible injury to his son, Mr. Samsa decides to be more patient and resolute with Gregor in the future and, along with his wife and daughter, tries to accept him as one of the family and not as the enemy. This change in Mr. Samsa does not necessarily suggest that Mr. Samsa's attitude toward Gregor has radically changed, but only that he is buying time and really doesn't know how to react to Gregor. Kafka does not explain this change in Mr. Samsa's thinking. It could be that now that he is working again and earning a salary and feels that he once again has the upper hand in the family, he is more willing to be accepting and patient with Gregor. Or it just may be that his focus is no longer primarily on his son, but on his job and on his wife and daughter. Distracted by these other cares and concerns, Mr. Samsa shows us that, if nothing else, he at least has the virtue of patience in his character.

In the evenings, the door to the living room is now left open all the time and this allows Gregor to listen in to his family's conversation when they are all seated around the table. From one of these conversations we learn that Mrs. Samsa has been employed by an underwear company as a seamstress, that Grete has taken a job as a salesgirl and is also studying French and learning shorthand to improve her prospects for the future. With all three members of the family now working, the family's finances seem to be improving. Gregor's parasitic life has forced his parents and sister to go to work and to become more independent. This new sign of their financial independence has two immediate benefits for them: it gives them a greater measure of personal freedom, and it diverts their attention away from Gregor, who had been their sole preoccupation for some time.

Gregor notices that in the evenings, when his father falls asleep in his chair, he still wears his bank messenger's uniform, as if he were about to go to work at a moment's notice. When the clock strikes 10, Gregor observes that his mother tries to rouse Mr. Samsa from his chair, but Mr. Samsa nods his head and then falls back to sleep again. At times, it takes Mrs. Samsa and Grete to lift Mr. Samsa out of his chair and practically carry him off to bed.

Comfortable, sleepy, and complacent, Mr. Samsa sometimes remarks, "This is a life. This is the peace and quiet of my old age." At this point, he shuffles off to bed, leaning on his wife and daughter for support. With the restoration of his position as head of the household, Mr. Samsa has finally found some peace and contentment in his old age. His trials and tribulations seem to be over, for Kafka gives us a picture of Mr. Samsa in this section that is in sharp contrast to the angry, vengeful father of Parts 1 and 2.

One day, a very tall, white-haired woman shows up in the apartment. This nameless cleaning woman takes on the responsibility of handling the heavy cleaning in the apartment mornings and evenings. The young servant girl, Anna, is no longer working for the Samsas and this new, older woman, a widow, has been engaged to free Mrs. Samsa and Grete from the more burdensome household tasks and duties. This old woman, whom Kafka describes as having white hair and a "strong bony frame" in effect becomes Gregor's undertaker. She will be the one to discover his body and to dispose of his corpse. Her appearance in the story is brief, but her function is unmistakable, and after she fulfills her function, she will be summarily dismissed by Mr. Samsa.

One evening, Gregor overhears his family discussing the pos-

sibility of moving to another, smaller apartment. Gregor is mentioned as the sole reason for their not being able to move out of their current apartment. How would they move Gregor out of his room? What would they do with him? Gregor knows only too well that he is not the reason for their lamentations and indecision. The real reason, he believes, is their own inertia, exhaustion, and feelings of hopelessness, and their conviction that they alone have been singled out by a cruel, unjust fate to deal with their terrible misfortune. All they have to do, Gregor reasons, if they really wanted to move, is to place Gregor into some kind of box with the necessary air holes in it for him to breathe, and they would be out of their apartment, but their despair and helplessness have paralyzed them. Further, they now have the extra burden of working and their jobs have physically drained them. Gregor watches his mother and sister at night, after they have put Mr. Samsa to bed, and sees them crying and wiping away their tears. His own sense of sorrow and guilt is enormous and overwhelms him, but his own ambivalence takes possession of him, too. His emotional life swings back and forth between guilt and rage and frustration. Although he feels directly responsible for his family's suffering, he also feels angry that they have chosen to neglect him completely. He sleeps little and refuses to eat anything at all. Often, Grete just shoves the food into his room with her foot and then returns with a broom to clear out the remains. She allows Gregor's room to turn into a dung heap, thick with dust and dust balls in every corner. The room that was once his only source of comfort, that provided him with a measure of safety and security, now threatens to engulf him with its gathering filth and fetid odors.

Mrs. Samsa can no longer tolerate the unhealthy condition of Gregor's room. One day she takes it upon herself to give the room a thorough cleaning. When Grete finds out what her mother has done, she grows furious with her and she reminds her that she alone has the responsibility of cleaning out Gregor's room. A big fight breaks out between the two women, and Mr. Samsa finally steps between them to settle the matter. He reprimands both his daughter and his wife for being at odds with each other, and he warns Grete never to clean Gregor's room again. Grete bursts into tears, while Mrs. Samsa quickly pulls Mr. Samsa toward the bedroom to calm him down. Meanwhile, Gregor is seething in his room. He hisses loudly at his family to show his displeasure and he reproaches them for not having the good sense to keep their squabbling and fighting to themselves.

These family eruptions—though more the exception than the rule—all point to the terrible pressure and the frayed nerves the family has been experiencing. Much of their private feelings—especially those of Grete and Mrs. Samsa—have been suppressed for a long time and occasionally their deepest emotions break through their stoic defenses—defenses that have been pierced by Gregor's helplessness and long suffering illness.

Here it might be interesting to note that while it is true that all this surging hostility and bitterness are seen through Gregor's eyes—indeed, the entire story is told from Gregor's point of view—it is also true that as his physical condition worsens and as his powers of observation diminish, his impressions are called into question. Can we be absolutely certain that what he is hearing and seeing is actually what is taking place? His body is weak, his vision is failing him, he sleeps little, and the little food he takes into his mouth is soon discharged. Lack of food over a long period of time usually results in a certain lightheadedness, if not a hallucinogenic state of mind, so we must ask ourselves how accurate Gregor's perceptions and observations of reality are. What is important is Gregor's sensitivity. Though his physical powers are weakening, his inner life or spiritual life has grown stronger. In this respect, we see growth and maturity in Gregor's character, and with growth comes recognition and understanding.

The old cleaning woman who has been placed in charge of cleaning out Gregor's room shows little reaction or emotion when she first lays eyes on Gregor. Perhaps her long, difficult life has prepared her for just this encounter with Gregor. Unlike the chief clerk, or Gregor's parents, this old charwoman seems to take things in stride. She is neither shocked nor horrified when she has to enter Gregor's room. She provides a little comic relief in the story by the way she calmly addresses him. She tries to humor him, and she speaks to him in a kind, friendly tone of voice, the way a grandmother might talk to her recalcitrant grandchild. "Come along then, you old dung beetle," she says.

Gregor, however, resents her intrusions and once, during a terrible rain, Gregor reacts violently and threatens to attack her when she enters his room and starts talking to him in her usual playful way. The cleaning woman picks up a chair and shows him that if he doesn't back away, she will bring it down on his head. This incident, though of relatively minor importance in the story, heightens Gregor's estrangement and demonstrates what happens when someone from outside the family is confronted with a repulsive-looking but harmless being.

Now that Grete has been replaced by the cleaning woman as Gregor's caretaker, Kafka tells us that "Gregor was now eating hardly anything." Is Gregor's absolute refusal to eat his way of passively withdrawing from life and the world? Or is this a form of self-imposed punishment for all the terrible hardships he has placed on his family? What better way to vanish from the world than by wasting away into nothingness?

With the entrance into the story of the three bearded lodgers who rent a room in the Samsa apartment, the story takes a subtle but important shift towards its climax. Kafka doesn't tell us who these men are. He gives them no names, he does not provide us with any facts of their lives or backgrounds. They are completely anonymous, each a carbon copy of the other. Who are these men and why does Kafka introduce them into the story precisely at this moment? Are they sinister characters, or do they have some divine purpose? Are they supposed to represent the Three Wise Men who come bearing "gifts" for Gregor's liberation and the Samsa family's salvation? Their full beards and serious demeanor might suggest three religious men—rabbis, perhaps—or teachers, but Kafka does not give them any calling or profession in life, so we are left to speculate on their significance. One thing is clear, as will be seen in Part 3, Division 2, and that is that they act as a catalyst and help push events toward their conclusion. By their idiosyncratic behavior, they generate a chain reaction of events that result in Gregor's death.

These three men are obsessed with cleanliness and order, and they force the cleaning woman to remove anything from their room that is superfluous to their needs. These things are deposited in Gregor's room, which begins to resemble an old storage room heaped with junk.

One evening, when the three lodgers are eating dinner, Gregor hears them chewing their food. He smells the plate of "steaming potatoes" and the rich, savory meat, and he sadly thinks, "How these lodgers are stuffing themselves, and here am I dying of starvation!" Like an old tired dog, whom the family no longer takes any delight or pleasure in, Gregor has been ignored, neglected, and left alone to suffer with his martyrdom, while the three bearded men become the main focus of the Samsa household.

Study Questions

1. How has Mr. Samsa's attitude toward Gregor changed at the start of Part 3, Division 1?

2. What kind of job does Mrs. Samsa have?

3. What kind of job does Grete have?

4. How is Grete trying to improve her prospects for the future?

5. How do you explain Grete's ambivalence toward Gregor?

6. Why does Grete become angry with her mother?

7. Who do the Samsas hire to clean Gregor's room?

8. Why do the Samsas rent a room to the three men?

9. Why doesn't Kafka give us any information about the three men?

10. How does Gregor feel when he hears the three men chewing their food at dinner?

Answers

1. Mr. Samsa decides to be more patient with Gregor, to suppress his real feelings toward Gregor, and not to regard him as the enemy.

2. Mrs. Samsa has taken a job sewing with an underwear company.

3. Grete has taken a job as a salesgirl.

4. Grete is studying French and learning shorthand in an attempt to secure a brighter, more financially rewarding future for herself.

5. Grete's ambivalence can best be explained by the fact that she begins to feel a loss of her own personal freedom in caring for Gregor and tending to his needs. She wants to help him and take care of him, but at the same time, she resents having to do so and probably realizes that her burden is robbing her of her youth and vitality.

6. Grete becomes angry with her mother when she finds out that Mrs. Samsa cleaned Gregor's room.

7. The Samsas hire an old woman, a widow, to come into the apartment mornings and evenings to clean up.

8. The Samsas rent a room to the three bearded men to earn more money and to divert their attention away from Gregor.

9. Kafka's intention in introducing the three men into the story is unclear. Perhaps the three men are symbols; however, the reader must interpret them within the context of the story. They are instrumental in forcing the story to its conclusion.

10. Gregor feels alone, desolate, and abandoned when he hears the three men chewing their food in the next room.

Suggested Essay Topics

1. It is clear from the outset of Part 3 that Gregor is dying. Write an essay explaining just how much of his physical decline is his own doing, and how much of it is caused by outside factors.

2. The three bearded lodgers who come into the story are intentionally made to be mysterious and anonymous. Use this section of the story to explain your thoughts and feelings about these three men. In your essay, consider the following factors: why they have no names, no distinguishing qualities or characteristics, no profession or background.

Part 3, Division 2

Summary

The action of Part 3, Division 2 begins with Gregor's emergence from his room during Grete's violin concert and ends with his death and the Samsa family's emotional and spiritual rebirth.

From his room, Gregor hears Grete's violin and sticks his head out of his room to listen. One of the lodgers notices him and immediately alerts Mr. Samsa. Mr. Samsa tries to assuage his boarders but one of the lodgers is so outraged at the sight of Gregor that he threatens to sue Mr. Samsa for damages and for causing him to live in such a close proximity to Gregor. The two other lodgers also protest their disgusting and inexcusable living conditions, and they threaten Mr. Samsa with a lawsuit as well, reminding him that they will not pay a penny for their room.

Because of this new crisis, Grete steps forward and takes matters into her own hands. She delivers an impassioned speech to her parents about the impossibility of living in the same apartment with Gregor. She argues that Gregor is no longer her brother and that he will some day drive them all into the gutter if he's allowed to get his way. She boldly suggests that they try to get rid of him, that his presence in the house is intolerable. Mr. Samsa nods and tacitly agrees with her. He tries to comfort her and soothe her worries, but he is at a loss as to the best way to dispose of Gregor.

Once Gregor returns to his room, he begins to feel a sense of relief. The pain in his back no longer bothers him, and although his whole body still aches, he feels comfortable, calm, and at peace with himself. He comes to the realization that Grete is probably right, that the best thing for him to do is disappear from their lives and to spare his family any further grief and heartache. He begins to think of his family with great affection and love. The only solution, he concludes, for all concerned, is for him simply to go away.

At three o'clock in the morning, with the clock chiming outside his window, Gregor takes his last breath and dies.

The following morning, the cleaning woman goes into Gregor's room. At first, she thinks he is sleeping and does not want to disturb him, but when she playfully pokes him with her broom, she

realizes that he is dead. She announces his death in a loud voice and then hurries to the Samsa bedroom to tell them the news.

Upon hearing the news of Gregor's death, Mr. Samsa thanks God, and then the three lodgers are brought to Gregor's room to see the corpse for themselves. After they have a look at the flattened body on the floor, the three lodgers are ordered to leave the apartment for good by Mr. Samsa. The cleaning woman assures Mr. and Mrs. Samsa that they have nothing to worry about, for she has already disposed of Gregor's body. After that, the cleaning woman is fired by Mr. Samsa.

The Samsa's decide to take a rest and inform their employers by letter that they are going on a short holiday. They board a train for the country. They fix their attention on Grete, who, despite her terrible ordeal of the last few months, has blossomed into an eligible, young, beautiful bride.

After what they have just endured, the Samsas' future looms bright and promising.

Analysis

The three lodgers are relaxing after dinner one night, smoking their cigars and reading their newspapers when they hear Grete's violin playing from the kitchen. Startled by the music, the three men rise in unison and move into another room, where they gather closely together and whisper to each other. Anxious that the three boarders might be offended by Grete's playing, Mr. Samsa asks them if her music is disturbing them, but they respond otherwise and insist that Grete continue playing for them in the room where they have just retired. The music stops momentarily while Mr. and Mrs. Samsa carry the music stand and the music into their room. Grete resumes playing for them, but this time the unpredictable lodgers express their displeasure with her playing and turn away from her, blowing cigar smoke all over the room.

In his room, Gregor hears the sweet music and is instantly drawn to it. The music has a soothing and profound effect on him. Looking out into the next room, he sees Grete's angelic expression as she plays, and he follows her face as she moves her eyes sadly to the notes coming from her violin. The extraordinary power of Grete's playing evokes warm, fond memories in Gregor and all the love and deep affection he once felt for his sister come flooding back into his heart. The music triggers one of Gregor's fantasies—to have his sister in his room all to himself. He imagines what it would be like if she came to his room to play just for him. He knows that she would not try to run away from him, but would remain with him while he guarded all the doors against all intruders. He would tell her again of his plans to send her away to the conservatory, and Grete would be so moved and thrilled by his generosity that she would break down and cry, and she would even allow him to kiss her on her bare neck.

While the incestuous nature of this fantasy cannot be overlooked, it is the anguish and despair, the loneliness and solitude that feed Gregor's illusions. Gregor is trying to recapture a world and a time that are no longer accessible to him. He pictures himself as Grete's hero, protecting her from outsiders and sending her to music school, but he can hardly defend himself, and his dream of enrolling her in the conservatory will never materialize. "He would never let her out of his room, at least, not so long as he lived." He would enjoy her playing, her companionship and friendship, and the physical intimacy, as evidenced by the "kiss on the neck," is a hunger born of sexual need and human affection and understanding.

Gregor's dream is soon shattered, and he is brought back to reality when one of the lodgers notices him in the doorway and points him out to Mr. Samsa.

Apprehensive, Mr. Samsa tries to mollify the lodger, but soon all three men are looking at Gregor in the doorway, more with amusement and curiosity than dismay. As Mr. Samsa tries to urge the three lodgers back into their room, the men become upset and angry, but it's not clear whether they are angry because of Mr. Samsa's sudden aggressive behavior or because they now fully realize that they have been sharing an apartment with a monstrous, repulsive insect and have been duped in some way.

One of the lodgers begins to protest that he has been swindled and deceived and, stamping his foot loudly and spitting on the floor, threatens to take Mr. Samsa to court for damages. Very soon, the two other lodgers join in the chorus of denunciation and they refuse to pay one penny for their room, given the disgusting and disgraceful conditions of the apartment. These threats stab Mr. Samsa in the heart and throw the whole household into utter chaos. All Mr. Samsa can do at this point is sink into his armchair and hold his twitching head in his hands, while the three lodgers scurry back to the safety of their room.

The air is charged with tension. Grete's violin, which has been resting in Mrs. Samsa's lap, falls to the floor with a resounding crash.

At this critical juncture, a sense of gloom descends upon the apartment. Seizing the opportunity, Grete is the first to speak as soon as the three men return to their room. She addresses her parents passionately, in a tone that is full of repressed anger and resentment. This is an important turning point in the story, both for Grete and for Gregor's fate.

Grete lets her parents know exactly how she feels about Gregor. She tells them that they can no longer go on living with Gregor, that he has become an imposition and a hindrance in their lives, that he will drive the lodgers away, and eventually, if he gets his way, put his family out on the street. More importantly, she no longer refers to Gregor as her brother, but uses the impersonal pronoun "it" when referring to him, and she speaks of him as a "creature" and not as a human being. For Grete, Gregor has become completely dehumanized and it is therefore easier for her to talk about the only solution left for them, namely, to just "get rid of him." This must be done without delay, she tells her parents. This flood of words comes pouring out of Grete; it is a spontaneous expression of her feelings. "He must go!" cries Grete. "That's the only solution, Father!"

Struggling with another asthma attack, Mrs. Samsa starts coughing, while Mr. Samsa can only nod in agreement with Grete's words.

Just as she is concluding her argument, Grete notices Gregor, and with some alarm, she points him out to her father, who quickly springs to his feet in a fit of anger and torment.

It is a little ironic that Grete, and not Mr. Samsa, should be the one to propose getting rid of Gregor, but it is Grete, and not her aging parents, who has the most to lose if they continue to accept the status quo at home. Grete has been the one who has witnessed Gregor's metamorphosis up close; she was the one who fed him

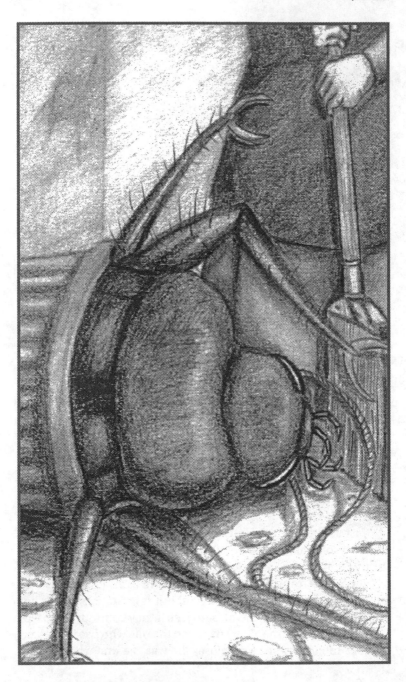

twice a day, cleaned up after him, and shouldered the responsibility of caring for him. Now she has no illusions about his recovery. She cannot, like her mother, pretend any longer that Gregor will one day return to his normal self and, like her father who seems to have settled into complacency and apathy, she cannot afford to remain passive and indifferent.

Her demand that Gregor "must go" seems heartless and cruel, but it is Grete who has the clarity of vision to see what is happening to her family. She worries about her mother's chronic asthma and is concerned about her father having to work, in his old age, as a bank messenger. More than that, she has her own life to think about now. She is growing older and will one day want to marry and raise a family. How can she ever receive young men in her apartment with that "creature" living in the next room? She is afraid of being consumed by Gregor's life, and so it is she who steps forward and speaks the unspeakable, and says that one thing that no one else has the courage to say—that Gregor must go.

After Gregor is spotted by his sister, he tries to turn around and go back to his room, but his sudden movement startles his family. A short silence follows during which time the family calms down and they watch Gregor from a safe distance in mournful silence. Mr. and Mrs. Samsa sit down heavily, as if life itself were crushing them with its cruel weight, while Grete looks on with great trepidation.

An eerie silence then sets in while Gregor crawls back to his room. No one speaks, no one stirs but Gregor, who is left entirely to himself. As he inches closer to the doorway of his room, he turns to see Grete, who has now risen to her feet. Gregor's last glance before entering his room is of his mother, and then Grete slams the door to his room after him. Pulling the key out of the door lock, she turns to her parents and says, "At last!"

With Gregor locked away in his room, the stage is now set for the story's denouement, or final resolution. Kafka carefully prepares Gregor's last scene for us with beatific, almost operatic detail. It is a little like the chorale movement of an orchestral work, where time itself seems to stand still.

Once Gregor is back in his room, he discovers that he feels more relaxed than ever before. Although his tired body is pulsating with pain, he seems to pay less attention to it now, a sure sign that his death is near. Even the rotting apple lodged in his back hardly bothers him anymore. Thoughts of death, and the comfort it will bring to his family, comfort Gregor in his last hour.

Gregor's thoughts turn to his family with increasing frequency during the night. His heart breaks and aches with love for them. In a flash, he realizes that Grete is right about him, that if he is to spare them further pain and anguish, he must simply "disappear." There is no other solution. With tender thoughts of his family in his head, Gregor dies just when the clock outside his window chimes three times. A great "broadening of light" enters his consciousness for the last time just before he expires.

The scene begins in darkness for Gregor and concludes with "the first broadening of light in the world outside his window" entering his consciousness. This suggests that Gregor's journey on earth—from child, to student, to traveling salesman to vermin— ends with Gregor's recognition or knowledge that his self-sacrifice is the greatest gift he can make to his family. The three chimes of the tower clock suggest the Holy Trinity and Gregor's salvation. While the entire death scene is "religious" in feeling, and while the religious symbolism may even suggest Gregor's resurrection or metamorphosis into a higher form of life, the reader should consider the scene from another perspective.

Gregor's death, like his life—like his metamorphosis—is dark and mysterious and inexplicable. Given his crippled, weak constitution, we know that he could not have lasted much longer in his present state. Gregor wills himself to die. He makes the supreme sacrifice for his family and in doing so, he has shed all mortal claims to his existence. The light that enters his consciousness is also the light that sets him free from his symbiotic relationship with his family. It allows him to slip away quietly from this earth and his death is neither painful nor full of torment, but rather something quite peaceful and beautiful and graceful. Like Grete's violin playing, which is his funeral dirge, the serenity of Gregor's death scene, with his acceptance that his struggle is finally over, has its own moving music. He lies in a "state of vacant and peaceful meditation," and his head sinks to the floor "of its own accord," and then from his nostrils come "the last faint flicker of his breath." These descriptions of Gregor's final moments give the scene a roundness and finality, and they suggest that Gregor's legacy—his self-sacrificing love—has meaning beyond his own mortal existence.

It is the old cleaning woman who discovers Gregor's body the following morning. After she is convinced that Gregor is indeed dead and not just sleeping, she runs to the Samsa bedroom to announce the news. Mr. Samsa thanks God for ending his long, painful ordeal, while Grete says, "Just see how thin he was. It's such a long time since he's eaten anything."

Grete follows her parents back into their bedroom after viewing Gregor's corpse. The three lodgers come out of their room to look at Gregor's body. Presently, the Samsas re-enter the living room. Mr. Samsa is wearing his bank messenger's uniform and he comes out with Grete on one arm, and his wife on his other. All appear to have been crying. Angrily, Mr. Samsa orders the three lodgers out of his house. The lodgers at first protest, but then they leave quietly.

The Samsas decide that it would be best if they took the day off from work and took a trip into the country. They all sit down and write letters to their employers explaining their intentions to take the day off to rest and to relax after their recent tragedy. As they are composing their letters, the cleaning lady reports to tell them that she has properly disposed of Gregor's body and that they have nothing to worry about in that regard. She attempts to explain just how this was done, but Mr. Samsa interrupts her, preferring to be spared the grisly details. After the cleaning woman leaves for the day, Mr. Samsa announces that that very night, she will be told to leave for good. Mrs. Samsa and Grete, though, are not listening to him. The cleaning woman disturbed their calm and they stand near the window, embracing and commiserating. Mr. Samsa says, "Let bygones be bygones. And you might have some consideration for me." Ever the self-centered egotist, Mr. Samsa's final words cut with a sharpness that is both icy and brutal, and remind us, in a cruel way, that life must go on.

While traveling to the country on the train, the Samsas take notice of their young daughter, and when the journey ends and Grete gets up out of her seat and stretches her "young body" the Samsas can't help but think that she is a very attractive young

woman who is fast approaching the age of marriage. They fix all their hopes for the future on her. The reader is left wondering if, now that Gregor is gone, the Samsas will now try to exploit their pretty young daughter and try to find her a husband who will provide for them in their declining old age.

Throughout the story, the reader is plunged into a dark, strange world turned nightmare, where the details of everyday life are sharply contrasted with the fantastic, often grotesque metamorphosis of Gregor Samsa. The ever shifting light in the story—from darkness to bright light—symbolizes the collision of these two worlds. With Gregor's death, the darkness recedes, and the Samsa apartment is flooded with a new light, "the first broadening of light in the world." It is also "the end of March" when Gregor dies, and there is a "certain softness" in "the air." Kafka makes it clear with these details that spring is very close and with spring comes renewal and rebirth.

Although *Metamorphosis* ends with Gregor's death, the theme of rebirth and regeneration is clearly apparent. From the family's enormous trial and suffering comes the promise of a better life and a brighter future for all.

Study Questions

1. Why do the three lodgers threaten to sue Mr. Samsa?

2. What private thoughts does Gregor have of Grete when he hears her violin playing?

3. Why does Grete want to get rid of Gregor?

4. How does Gregor feel once he is back in his room?

5. How would you describe the cleaning woman's responses to Gregor when she first comes into the house?

6. Why does Gregor feel that Grete is right about his disappearing from everyone's life?

7. Who discovers Gregor's body?

8. Why does Mr. Samsa order the three lodgers out of the house?

9. What do the Samsas plan to do the day of Gregor's death?

10. In what sense is *Metamorphosis* an "optimistic" story?

Answers

1. When it is clear to the three lodgers that they have been living with a disgusting insect in the same apartment, they threaten to sue Mr. Samsa for the disgusting and intolerable conditions that prevail in the household.

2. Gregor fantasizes that Grete will come to his room and play for him alone. He dreams that he will never let her out of his room, that he will guard all the doors against intruders and outsiders, and that Grete will be so happy and thrilled by his promise to send her to music school that she would allow him to kiss her on her bare neck. It is an heroic fantasy, where Gregor sees himself as Grete's hope, protector, and salvation, roles he was never able to fulfill in life.

3. Grete realizes that Gregor is no longer her brother; she speaks of him as a "creature" and uses the impersonal pronoun "it" when referring to him. She tells her parents that they must find a way to "get rid of him"; otherwise he will surely drive all of them into the gutter.

4. Once Gregor returns to his room, a feeling of calm comes over him. His aching body no longer troubles him. He is more relaxed and serene, less agitated. His thoughts turn to death.

5. The cleaning woman reacts with a sense of amusement and curiosity when she first lays eyes on Gregor. She displays neither fear nor horror at the sight of him but seems to accept him just as he is.

6. Gregor comes to realize that the only solution for him and for his family is for him to disappear, that is, to die. Only in that way, will his family be happy again and be able to resume their lives as before.

7. The cleaning woman is the first to discover Gregor's corpse.

8. The sight of the three lodgers standing in Gregor's doorway and looking down at the flattened body of his son angers Mr. Samsa enough to want them out of his house. It is a spon-

taneous, human reaction that probably expresses Mr.
Samsa's latent hostility for the three lodgers.

9. On the day of Gregor's death, the Samsas decide to take a
long deserved rest and plan to take a trip to the country to
relax. They each write their employers telling them of their
intentions to do just that.

10. *Metamorphosis* can be regarded as an "optimistic" story for
a few reasons. Spring is the season of rebirth and renewal.
The car they are riding in is "filled with warm sunshine,"
suggesting a brighter future, and Gregor's death, though by
no means senseless, results in a renewal of the family's
dreams and hopes.

Suggested Essay Topics

1. The theme of physical decay and illness is a prominent
theme in the story. Write an essay tracing Gregor's physical
decline from the beginning of Part 3, Division 2, until his
death.

2. Write a paper in which you contrast Gregor's state of mind
at the beginning of this section to right before his death.
What incidents or events cause a change in Gregor's attitude
and thinking? Are Gregor's thoughts rational and clear, or
are they blurred and irrational?

SECTION THREE

Sample Analytical Paper Topics

Metamorphosis is a richly layered and textured story that is open to many interpretations, that is, religious, philosophical, autobiographical, Freudian, and mythical, to name a few. The following paper topics contain a thesis statement, and an outline should be used to stimulate your thinking and writing about the story.

Topic #1

The term metamorphosis means a complete and profound change in form, structure, and substance or a change in form from one stage to the next in the life of an organism. The central change in *Metamorphosis* is the change in Gregor's life, from an ordinary man and traveling salesman to a gigantic insect. Gregor's transformation causes other remarkable changes in the story—changes that directly bear on his family. Write a paper that shows how Gregor's major change in life also affects the lives of his parents and sister.

Outline

I.   Thesis Statement: *Change is the essence of life, and in* Metamorphosis, *the theme of change is organic to the action, dictating the unfolding of the plot and influencing the characters' behavior and destiny.*

II. Initial change in Gregor's life: his metamorphosis into a gigantic insect and the thoughts, reflections, and feelings this profound change causes in him on the first day.

    A.   Gregor's conscious awareness that he has become an insect and the thoughts and feelings this discovery evoke in him

    B.   The familiar sights and objects in Gregor's room and how these objects are contrasted to the extreme circumstances he finds himself in

    C.   Gregor's chief concern, his job; the fact that he's missed his early morning train, and his fear that someone from his office may come to check on him

    D.   The response of the chief clerk and his parents as he shows himself to them for the first time

III.   Second change in Gregor's life: his adjustment to his new body, to his new life as an insect

    A.   Recognizing the limitations of his body; his loss of appetite for milk, his private feelings for his sister

    B.   Feelings of guilt and sorrow when he overhears his father discussing the family's plight and financial situation

    C.   The effect the removal of his furniture has on his spirit; changes in Grete as she cares for him

    D.   How Gregor's helplessness affects Mr. Samsa and how this changes the balance of power in the house

    E.   Gregor's futile attempt to placate his father's anger and his hapless retreat to his room when he is being bombarded with apples

    F.   His mother's desperate screams and pleas to spare Gregor's life when she runs to her husband

IV.   Third change in Gregor's life and in that of his family: complete reversal of family roles, that is, the family no longer depends on Gregor for their support, while Gregor must now depend on his family for his survival

    A.   The different jobs the family takes to earn money

    B.   Grete's increasing ambivalence toward Gregor

    C.   Gregor's decline in health; his slide into disintegration and decay

    D.   The domino effect the three lodgers have on the plot and on Gregor's fate

V.   The change in the family fortunes after Gregor's death

    A.   Hope and renewal symbolized by the coming of spring, the warm sunshine in the train, Grete's youthful, attractive body

    B.   Grete's own metamorphosis into a young, beautiful eligible bride

Topic #2

Other short stories have been written in which the central character's dying and death have a lasting effect on those around him or her. One such story is Leo Tolstoy's *The Death of Ivan Ilych* (1884). Compare and contrast the two stories, focusing on how the protagonist of each story, Gregor Samsa and Ivan Ilych, affect their families through their strange illnesses.

Outline

I.   Thesis Statement: *Both Gregor Samsa and Ivan Ilych share the same unfortunate fate in that both suffer an irreversible illness that deeply affects their families' lives.*

II.   Gregor Samsa and Ivan Ilych: their lives compared and contrasted before and after their illnesses

    A.   Gregor's life as a traveling salesman and Ivan Ilych's life as a magistrate

    B.   Gregor's initial response to his metamorphosis and Ivan Ilych's denial that there is something wrong with him

    C.   Gregor's mild acceptance of his fate and Ivan Ilych's refusal to accept the pain in his side and the fact that he may be dying

    D.   Initial family reactions: Gregor's family is one of shock and horror and sorrow; Ivan Ilych's family's indifference to what has happened to him

III. The way Gregor's regressive behavior impacts his family and the manner in which Ivan Ilych's illness torments his wife and children

    A. The general torpor that settles over the Samsa family and the annoyance Ivan Ilych's family experiences when they hear him scream out

    B. The way Kafka and Tolstoy both describe the banality of everyday life and its contrast to the acute suffering, both mental and physical, of the protagonists

    C. How Mr. Samsa and his wife and daughter change in their attitudes toward Gregor, and the way Ivan Ilych's wife and children show their resentment and irritation toward Ivan Ilych's illness

    D. Grete's change of heart, her self-importance, and self-possession and ambivalent feelings toward Gregor

IV. The changes induced in both Gregor and Ivan Ilych as they come to the end of their lives

    A. Ivan Ilych's internal, mental suffering compared to Gregor Samsa's inner thoughts and feelings as he approaches death

    B. Ivan Ilych's talk with the peasant, Gerasim, contrasted to Gregor's ongoing inner dialogue to find meaning and truth

    C. Ivan Ilych's spiritual growth and understanding compared to Gregor's resignation and sense of hopelessness

V. Ivan Ilych's understanding of the meaning of his life and inevitable death compared to Gregor Samsa's tender feelings of love for his parents and sister

    A. Ivan Ilych's self-knowledge and revelation

    B. Gregor Samsa's moment of clarity before death

    C. The Samsa family's new life

    D. Ivan Ilych's forgiveness, his love for his family

    E. The peaceful deaths of both protagonists

Topic #3

Symbolism often appears in modern literature as a name, event, action, or object that embodies more than its literal, concrete meaning. Like many of Kafka's works, *Metamorphosis* is rich in its symbolism. Symbolism allows the reader to penetrate the complexity and mystery of a work of art with greater understanding and insight. Discuss the symbolism in *Metamorphosis*. Try to focus on only those symbols that you think may have relevance to the story's ideas and themes and characters.

Outline

I.   Thesis Statement: *The symbolism found in* Metamorphosis *helps us to understand Gregor's inner life better and illuminates the conflicts he experiences after his metamorphosis.*

II. Gregor's transformation into a repellent, gigantic insect

    A.   Why an insect? Why not something equally repugnant or noxious? A vulture? A rat? A poisonous snake? Would the story be any different if Gregor turned into one of the above?

    B.   The many doors in the Samsa apartment and what they mean when they're open and closed

    C.   The importance of the story beginning just before Christmas and ending right before spring

    D.   The familiar sights in Gregor's room and how they're related to his life as a salesman and student

    E.   The significance of the chief clerk and what he comes to represent in Gregor's life

III. Intensification of the father-son relationship

    A.   Gregor's life as a salesman and as the family breadwinner before his metamorphosis

    B.   Mr. Samsa's life before and after his business failed

    C.   Gregor's increasing reliance and dependency on his father; his fear of his father; the love he has for his mother

D. The importance of the picture of the woman in her furs; Gregor's attachment to it, his fierce desire to protect it at any cost

E. Mr. Samsa's bank uniform, the gold buttons

F. The apples used by Mr. Samsa to attack Gregor

G. The way Mrs. Samsa flings herself on Mr. Samsa in a state of near undress

IV. The arrival of the cleaning woman and the number "three"

A. The cleaning woman's white hair, her age, the fact that she's a widow

B. The use of the number "three" in the story: three chimes of the clock, three lodgers, the appearance of Gregor three times outside his room, the three members of the Samsa family, the structure of the story into three parts, the three months from late December to early March—the span of the story itself

C. The cleaning woman's discovery of Gregor's body; her disposal of his body

D. The cleaning woman's dismissal

E. The religious significance of the number "three"

SECTION FOUR

Bibliography

Quotations of *Metamorphosis* are taken from the following edition:

Selected Short Stories of Franz Kafka. Trans. Willa and Edwin Muir. New York: The Modern Library, 1936.

Other Sources:

Albérès, R.M. and Pierre De Boisdeffre. *Kafka: The Torment of Man*. Trans. Wade Baskin. New York: The Citadel Press, 1968.

Brod, Max. *Franz Kafka: A Biography*. Trans. G. Humphreys Roberts and Richard Winston. New York: Schocken Books, 1963.

Carrouges, Michel. *Kafka Versus Kafka*. Trans. Emmett Parker. University of Alabama Press, 1968.

Gray, Ronald. ed., *Kafka: A Collection of Critical Essays*. Englewood Cliffs, NJ: Prentice-Hall, Inc. 1962.

Kafka, Franz. *Letter to His Father*. New York: Schocken Books, 1954.

Pawel, Ernst. *The Nightmare of Reason: A Life of Franz Kafka*. New York: Vintage Books, 1985.

Taikeff, Stanley. *The Hermit of Prague: A Dramatic Monologue*. Middletown, N.Y.: Whitlock Press, Inc. 1985.

Available at your local bookstore or order directly from us by sending in coupon below.